Michelle

From:

Zeni

Date:

2/27/15

Circle of Friends is a ministry of women helping women. Born out of a small accountability group that led to a women's Bible study, Circle of Friends Ministries is now a nonprofit organization dedicated to encouraging women to find and follow Christ. Our desire is to encourage one another to love God more deeply and to follow Him with a heart of passion that reaches out and draws others along with us on our journey.

> "Circle of Friends are women of
> biblical depth and compassion for others.
> They have a knack for bringing humor, hope,
> and practical application to everyday situations."

—Carol Kent, speaker and author, *When I Lay My Isaac Down* and *A New Kind of Normal*

> "Circle of Friends has its finger on the pulse
> of the heart-needs of women today.
> Through word and song they link arms
> with women around the globe to bring
> the hope and healing of Jesus Christ."

—Sharon Jaynes, speaker and author

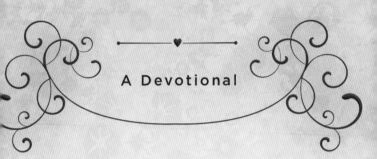

A Devotional

Encouragement
and Hope for a
Woman's Heart

BARBOUR BOOKS
An Imprint of Barbour Publishing, Inc.

© 2014 by Barbour Publishing, Inc.

Print ISBN 978-1-62836-964-9

eBook editions:
Adobe Digital Edition (.epub) 978-1-63058-624-9
Kindle and MobiPocket Edition (.prc) 978-1-63058-625-6

Scripture quotations marked NASB are taken from the New American Standard Bible, © 1960, 1962, 1963, 1968, 1971, 1972, 1973, 1975, 1977, 1995 by The Lockman Foundation. Used by permission.

Scripture quotations marked NIV are taken from the HOLY BIBLE, NEW INTERNATIONAL VERSION®. NIV®. Copyright © 1973, 1978, 1984, 2011 by Biblica, Inc.™ Used by permission. All rights reserved worldwide.

Scripture quotations marked NLT are taken from the *Holy Bible*. New Living Translation copyright© 1996, 2004, 2007 by Tyndale House Foundation. Used by permission of Tyndale House Publishers, Inc. Carol Stream, Illinois 60188. All rights reserved.

Scripture quotations marked KJV are taken from the King James Version of the Bible.

Scripture quotations marked AMP are taken from the Amplified® Bible, © 1954, 1958, 1962, 1964, 1965, 1987 by The Lockman Foundation. Used by permission.

Scripture quotations marked NKJV are taken from the New King James Version®. Copyright © 1982 by Thomas Nelson, Inc. Used by permission. All rights reserved.

Scripture quotations marked CEV are from the Contemporary English Version, Copyright © 1995 by American Bible Society. Used by permission.

Scripture quotations marked ESV are from The Holy Bible, English Standard Version®, copyright © 2001 by Crossway Bibles, a publishing ministry of Good News Publishers. Used by permission. All rights reserved.

Scripture quotations marked NRSV are taken from the New Revised Standard Version Bible, copyright 1989, Division of Christian Education of the National Council of the Churches of Christ in the United States of America. Used by permission. All rights reserved.

Scripture quotations marked MSG are from *THE MESSAGE*. Copyright © by Eugene H. Peterson 1993, 1994, 1995, 1996, 2000, 2001, 2002. Used by permission of NavPress Publishing Group.

Scripture quotations marked NCV are taken from the New Century Version of the Bible, copyright © 2005 by Thomas Nelson, Inc. Used by permission. All rights reserved.

Cover design by Kirk Douponce, DogEared Design

Published by Barbour Books, an imprint of Barbour Publishing, Inc., P.O. Box 719, Uhrichsville, Ohio 44683, www.barbourbooks.com

Our mission is to publish and distribute inspirational products offering exceptional value and biblical encouragement to the masses.

Member of the
Evangelical Christian
Publishers Association

Printed in China.

Share a Little Hope and Encouragement Today

Who can understand the heart of a woman—with all its joys and triumphs, challenges and heartaches—better than another woman? We are told in Titus that mature women of the faith are able to be "teachers of good things," and in Hebrews that we are to "exhort (encourage) one another daily."

Encouragement and Hope for a Woman's Heart is a daily devotional written by women who have a passion and love for Jesus. Their stories, insights, biblical applications, and their refreshing honesty in everyday trials in their lives will encourage your heart and strengthen your faith. So grab a cup of coffee or tea, pull up a chair, and share life, share hope, with your "Circle of Friends." You'll laugh, you'll cry, you'll find that you have truly found a place to belong. . . .

Hope in Suffering

"But I have this against you, that you have left your first love."

REVELATION 2:4 NASB

One of my favorite questions to ask couples over dinner is "How did you meet?" Each story invariably presents a set of impossible circumstances that had to be orchestrated in order to bring this man and woman together. As these details are relayed, a glow begins to come back into the eyes of those remembering. There is nothing to compare with that "first bloom of love."

This is the kind of love which God desires from us. That on-fire, totally consuming, single focus of our attention. His call to the church at Ephesus then was that they remember their first love—and rekindle their purpose to seek Him first.

His message, however, to the church at Smyrna was very different. " 'I know your tribulation and your poverty (but you are rich). . . Do not fear what you are about to suffer. . . . Be faithful until death, and I will give you the crown of life' " (Revelation 2:9–10 NASB).

Throughout history, God's church has suffered persecution. But here is a message of hope to all for whom cruelty is a constant companion: "Remain faithful, God's reward is at hand."

Carol L. Fitzpatrick
Daily Wisdom for Women

Mountain Ranges

God is our refuge and strength,
an ever-present help in trouble.

PSALM 46:1 NIV

D o you see clearly? Are you able to view things from under the fog you are in? I have been in that place far more often than I would like to admit. Things discourage me and cause me to want to give up and walk away. Sometimes I feel as though all I ever do is walk over that same mountain range day in and day out. It feels like I will never get to the end and walk on flat land again.

Have you ever been that discouraged?

Admit it! Be honest.

This morning when I woke up after yet another trip across that mountain range, I received this scripture from one of my sons. He sent it to me in a very simple e-mail. Then he said, "I love you." Amazing how those three little words can speak volumes. I received them from my son, but as I write this, I realize that they were from God! The above scripture is the reference my son sent. He knows me well. He knows that when my heart is fearful, when I am feeling overwhelmed, I need to be reminded that God is with me and that I will not fall. That He will help me at the break of day. Yes, my friends, God is there; and more than that, He loves you!

Becki Reiser
Circle of Friends

Divine Appointments

Jesus said, "Take care of my sheep."

JOHN 21:16 NIV

A beautiful young woman stumbled into the airplane obviously exhausted. She was dressed in skintight jeans, a distracting, low-cut T-shirt, and sunglasses that hid something. . .but I wasn't sure what.

"They messed up my ticket, and I don't have a seat," she complained to the flight attendant.

"This one's empty," I offered, pointing to the seat next to me.

I pulled out my book, *Your Scars Are Beautiful to God*, to prepare for an upcoming interview, but I sensed God saying, *Put down the book and talk to this girl.*

God, she doesn't want to talk, I argued.

Put down the book and talk to this girl.

I put down my book and turned to my fellow passenger.

"Where are you headed?" I asked.

"Home."

"Where's home?"

"A small town I'm sure you've never heard of."

Then she glanced down at the book in my lap.

"Scars. Well, I've certainly got a lot of those."

"So do I," I said. "That's why I wrote the book."

"You wrote it?" She was surprised.

For the next hour and a half, this young girl poured out her heart to me. She had been abandoned, sexually abused, and misused. As I prayed for her, tears spilled down her cheeks to wash away the years of regret.

We parted ways, but the memory lingered. God allowed me to apply His healing salve to the wounds of one of His little lambs.

There was no mix-up in her airline ticket; she had a divine seat assignment made by God.

Sharon Jaynes
Extraordinary Moments with God

God's Blueprint for This Moment

"So don't worry about tomorrow,
for tomorrow will bring its own worries.
Today's trouble is enough for today."

MATTHEW 6:34 NLT

The battle always has to be fought before the victory is won, though many people think they must have the victory before the battle. The conflict with worry and fear is almost always there—each person must overcome or be overcome. But we must fight each battle of our lives in the strength of Jesus' victory. He said, "As the Father has sent me, I am sending you" (John 20:21 NIV). We are to be like Jesus—One of whom Satan is afraid!

When we worry, we are carrying tomorrow's load with today's strength; carrying two days in one. We are moving into tomorrow ahead of time. There is just one day in the calendar of action—today. The Holy Spirit does not give a clear blueprint of our whole lives, but only of the moments, one by one.

We all have the same enemies—we are all preyed upon by frustration and worry. In India, Australia,

Japan, Germany—we need the same Holy Spirit. We need to remember that we are children of God, living within His constant care. God knows and is interested both in the hardest problems we face and the tiniest details that concern us. He knows how to put everything in place, like a jigsaw puzzle, to make a beautiful picture.

Corrie ten Boom
He Cares for You

A New Song

Sing a new song to the LORD,
for he has done wonderful deeds.
His right hand has won a mighty victory;
his holy arm has shown his saving power!

PSALM 98:1 NLT

Who needs a new song? Do you ever get tired of the old tune? I do! A new song! Spiritually, many of us need a new song to sing. Some of us are sung out, tired of singing solo or of being lost in a big choir where no one notices our contribution! God can give us a new song to sing. It will start when we meet with God and tune in to the vibrations of heaven. Songs you've never sung before have a fresh, sweet, winsome sound that alerts those around you to the state of your soul. God gave me a new song when my children got married, when my husband had to be away a lot, and when I got sick and had to have a scary operation. They were new songs because I'd never been in those situations, and new situations require new songs. They were not always happy songs, but who says all songs are happy ones? A minor key can be just as pretty as a major one.

The important thing is to sing a song—a new song of faith and hope, of self-discovery or God-discovery, at every turn of the road, every station, every resting place. Just today I asked Him to help me find something to sing about as I washed up a pile of dirty dishes. He helped me to compose a new song over the kitchen sink. God is never stuck for a tune. New songs are the Spirit's business—ask Him to give you one.

Jill Briscoe
The One Year Book of Devotions for Women

Without a Doubt

"I have loved you with
an everlasting love."

JEREMIAH 31:3 NIV

I remember once seeing the indignation of a mother I knew, stirred to its very depths by a little doubting on the part of one of her children. She had brought two little girls to my house to leave them while she did some errands. One of them, with the happy confidence of childhood, abandoned herself to all the pleasures she could find in my nursery and sang and played until her mother's return.

The other one, with the wretched caution and mistrust of maturity, sat down alone in a corner to wonder whether her mother would remember to come back for her, and to fear she would be forgotten, and to imagine her mother would be glad of the chance to get rid of her anyhow, because she was such a naughty girl, and ended with working herself up into a perfect frenzy of despair.

The look on that mother's face, when upon her return the weeping little girl told what was the matter with her, I shall not easily forget. Grief, wounded love, indignation, and pity all strove together for mastery. But indignation gained the day, and I doubt if that little girl was ever so vigorously dealt with before.

A hundred times in my life since has that scene come up before me with deepest teaching and has compelled me, peremptorily, to refuse admittance to the doubts about my heavenly Father's love and care and remembrance of me that have clamored at the door of my heart for entrance.

Hannah Whitall Smith
The Christian's Secret of a Happy Life

Hope of Better Things

Still another said, "I will follow you, Lord; but first let me go back and say goodbye to my family." Jesus replied, "No one who puts a hand to the plow and looks back is fit for service in the kingdom of God."

LUKE 9:61–62 NIV

Jesus had "resolutely set out for Jerusalem" (verse 51) but several of His followers failed to count the cost of discipleship. Jesus knew this man who wanted to first "go back" to his family had a longing for his old life. No one can move in two directions at once. It is impossible to go forward when you are looking to the past. A man who plows a field looking over his shoulder plows a crooked furrow, which means disaster for the whole field.

Jesus calls us to set our minds, our wills, and our hearts to follow Him. If we live with a divided mind or heart, longing for the things of this world, we will end up like the rich man in Luke 18:22 who "went away sorrowful." He loved his life of wealth more than he loved the Lord and could not commit to following Him.

To be fit for His service, to join the fellowship of His followers, we must first let go of anything we hold in more esteem than our Savior. When our fists are tightly clutched around our own plans and longings, we lose out on what God wants to give us. We need to open our hand, release everything, and allow God to fill our lives with something better—His plan for us.

Missy Horsfall
Circle of Friends

The Promise of Joy

Weeping may endure for a night,
but joy cometh in the morning.

PSALM 30:5 KJV

Have you experienced suffering? Perhaps you are hurting even now. Tough times are a reality for all of us.

The psalmist David was well acquainted with hardship. He used phrases such as "the depths," "the pit," and even "the grave" to describe them. Although he was known as a man after God's own heart, at times David was pursued by his enemies and forced to run for his life. He also lived with the consequences of committing murder and adultery, even long after receiving God's forgiveness.

God is faithful, and suffering is temporary. This is a promise we can claim, as David did, when facing difficulty or depression. David experienced God's faithfulness throughout the ups and downs of his life.

King Solomon, one of the wisest men who ever lived, concludes in the third chapter of Ecclesiastes that there is a time for everything, including "a time to weep and a time to laugh" (v. 4 NIV).

Some trials are short lived. Others are more complex. As believers, we can find joy in the Lord even as certain trials remain a backdrop in our lives. All suffering will end one day when we meet Jesus. The Bible assures us that in heaven there will be no tears.

Your loving heavenly Father has not forgotten you. You may feel that relief will never come, but take courage. It will.

Emily Biggers
Whispers of Wisdom for Busy Women

The King's Prosperity

A King shall reign and prosper.

JEREMIAH 23:5 KJV

If we are really interested, heart and soul, in a person, how delighted we are to have positive assurance of his prosperity, and how extremely interested and pleased we feel at hearing anything about it! Is not this a test of our love to our King? Are we both interested and happy in the short, grand, positive words which are given us about His certain prosperity? If so, the pulse of our gladness is beating true to the very heart of God.

If we could get one glimpse of our King in His present glory and joy, how we who love Him would rejoice for Him and with Him! And if we could get one great view of the wide but hidden prosperity of His kingdom at this moment, where would be our discouragement and faintheartedness! Many Christians nowadays are foregoing an immense amount of cheer, because they do not take the trouble to inquire, or read, or go where they can hear about the present prosperity of His kingdom. Those who do not care much can hardly be loving much or helping much.

But we do care about it; and so how jubilantly the promises of His increasing prosperity ring out to us!

Frances Ridley Havergal
Daily Thoughts for the King's Children

The Most Beautiful
Woman in the World

They saw that his face was radiant.
Then Moses would put the veil back
over his face until he went in
to speak with the LORD.

EXODUS 34:35 NIV

Film legend Audrey Hepburn was named the most naturally beautiful woman of all time by a panel of experts in June 2004. Hepburn topped the poll of beauty editors, makeup artists, fashion editors, model agencies, and fashion photographers who were asked to choose their top ten beauties from the list of one hundred compiled on www.smh.com. The women were chosen for their "embodiment of natural beauty, healthy living, beautiful on the inside and out, with great skin and a natural glow to their personality, as well as their complexion."

The article went on to say that Hepburn is the personification of natural beauty because "she has a rare charm and inner beauty that radiates when she smiles. Her skin looks fresh in all her films, and her personality really shines through as someone warm and lively."

Did you notice that Audrey Hepburn's inner beauty was mentioned twice in the judges' reasoning for choosing her? Sure, there were many other beauties who made the list. Some may have been even more beautiful than Hepburn, but apparently their inner beauty was found lacking, even though their exterior beauty was striking.

That's good news, isn't it? That means even if our skin isn't flawless and even if our teeth aren't perfectly straight, we can still "radiate beauty" because of our gorgeous inner looks.

Spend some time with God today, and get a makeover by the Master. Soon you'll radiate His love, and people will find you attractive.

Michelle Medlock Adams
Secrets of Beauty

I Think I Can

I can do all this through
him who gives me strength.

PHILIPPIANS 4:13 NIV

Remember the Little Golden Book about the little engine that could? You know the story. He tries really hard—against many odds—chugging along and puffing, "I think I can, I think I can" until he proves everyone wrong and reaches his goal. I've always loved that little book. You know why? Because it's packed with powerful teaching. If we can keep a can-do attitude, we can achieve many things.

My eleven-year-old daughter, Abby, is a great gymnast. In fact, she is a member of a competitive gymnastics team. When Abby is preparing for her tumbling pass, I can always tell if she's going to do well just by the look on her face. If she approaches the mat with a can-do facial expression, I know she's going to nail it. But if she shows fear on her face, I know she's not going to give her best performance. It's all in the attitude.

Maybe you have a goal that seems impossible to

reach—sort of like the little engine that could. Well, God says that you can do all things through Him, so go for it! Keep a can-do attitude, and watch your dreams become a reality!

Michelle Medlock Adams
Daily Wisdom for Working Women

The Center of Life

Six days thou shalt labour, and do
all thy work: but the seventh day is
the sabbath of the LORD thy God:
in it thou shalt not do any work.

DEUTERONOMY 5:13–14 KJV

Workaholics, beware! Don't expect God to sanction your seven-day workweek.

God did not mean our jobs to be everyday things. We wear out emotionally and spiritually if we focus continually on work. Worse than that, it quickly becomes our god. When we become too wrapped up in our careers, the place He is designed for—the center of our lives—becomes filled with thoughts of how we can cram more labor into our days, get things done, and improve our status in the company. Before long, we're empty and tired. We've been grasping at straws, and suddenly we find a hayrack in our hands, not the success we'd looked for.

Life without God is empty. So take a day of rest, worship God, and get your life in focus. Give God His proper place, and life will go more smoothly. You'll find success, even if it's not in the place you expected it.

Lord, I need to keep You in the center of my life. Help me spend Sunday worshipping You, not focusing on the things I "need" to accomplish.

Pamela L. McQuade
Daily Wisdom for the Workplace

The Nature of Comfort

My comfort in my suffering is this:
Your promise preserves my life.

PSALM 119:50 NIV

Comfort, whether human or divine, is pure and simple comfort and is nothing else. We none of us care for pious phrases. We want realities; and the reality of being comforted and comfortable seems to me almost more delightful than any other thing in life. We all know what it is. When as little children we have cuddled up into our mother's lap after a fall or a misfortune, and have felt her dear arms around us and her soft kisses on our hair, we have had comfort. When as grown-up people after a hard day's work we have put on our slippers and seated ourselves by the fire, in an easy chair with a book, we have had comfort. When after a painful illness we have begun to recover and have been able to stretch our limbs and open our eyes without pain, we have had comfort. When someone whom we dearly love has been ill almost unto death and has been restored to us in health again, we have had comfort. A thousand times in our lives probably have we said, with a sigh of relief, as of toil over or burdens laid off, "Well this is comfortable," and in that word *comfortable* there has been comprised more of rest, and relief, and satisfaction, and pleasure, than any other word glory of the religion of the Lord Jesus Christ.

He was anointed to comfort "all that mourn." The "God of all comfort" sent His Son to be the comforter of a mourning world. And all through His life on earth He fulfilled His divine mission. The God of all Comfort enfolds life's trials and pains in an all-embracing peace.

Hannah Whitall Smith
The God of All Comfort

Ready to Fly

He brought me out into a
spacious place; he rescued me
because he delighted in me.

PSALM 18:19 NIV

Many of us live busy, lonely lives. We can be surrounded by people, even family, and still feel isolated and alone. It's risky to be known. What if in a moment of finally stepping out of our cocoon, ready to spread our wings and fly, someone laughs at us—or worse still, simply turns her back and continues with her conversation? When a child is born and the very first face she focuses on is the face of her adoring mother, part of the rip of Eden is healed. When that love and acceptance are further strengthened through the years by her father, and by family and friends, it will be hard to convince this little one that she is not worth loving. The trouble with the human experience of many is that the love they needed and craved as a child was withheld, and the tear of separation that began in Eden has gotten bigger. One of the greatest spiritual gifts of rebirth when we give our lives to

Christ is that we have fresh eyes to look into and see how much we are treasured. You have a Father who adores you, who delights in your laugh, who celebrates your gifts, and who catches every tear that falls from your eyes. His love will give you the courage to leave the cocoon behind and fly.

Sheila Walsh
Let Go

A Grand Promise

Uphold me according to your
promise, that I may live, and let me
not be put to shame in my hope.

PSALM 119:116 NRSV

Perhaps there is no point in which expectation has
been so limited by experience as this. We believe
God is able to do for us just so much as He has already
done, and no more. We take it for granted a line must
be drawn somewhere; and so we choose to draw it
where experience ends, and faith would have to begin.
Even if we have trusted and proved Him as to keeping our members and our minds, faith fails when we
would go deeper and say, "Keep my will!" And the
result of this, as of every other faithless conclusion, is
either discouragement and depression, or, still worse,
acquiescence in an unyielded will, as something that
can't be helped.

Now let us turn from our thoughts to God's
thoughts. Verily, they are not as ours! He says He is
able to do exceedingly abundantly above all that we
ask or think. Apply this here.

We ask Him to take our wills and make them His. Does He or does He not mean what He says? And if He does, should we not trust Him to do this thing that we have asked and longed for, and not less, but more? Is anything too hard for the Lord? Hath He said, and shall He not do it? Does He mock our longing by acting as I have seen an older person act to a child, by accepting some trifling gift of no intrinsic value, just to please the little one, and then throwing it away as soon as the child's attention is diverted? We give Him no opportunity (so to speak) of proving His faithfulness to this great promise, but we will not fulfill the condition of reception, believing it.

It is most comforting to remember that the grand promise, "Thy people shall be willing in the day of Thy power," is made by the Father to Christ Himself. The Lord Jesus holds this promise, and God will fulfill it to Him. He will make us willing because He has promised Jesus He will do so.

Frances Ridley Havergal
Kept for the Master's Use

Listen and Reflect

As often as possible Jesus withdrew
to out-of-the-way places for prayer.

LUKE 5:16 MSG

The time is short. Listen carefully to My words. Hide them in your heart, for they need a time for developing within you, even as seeds that are planted in the earth. My Word needs a period to rest quietly within your heart until it is quickened by the Spirit. Then shall it rise in newness of life. In this way I will bring forth through you new truth and fresh revelation.

No new truth can be generated in the midst of activity. New life springs from the placid pools of reflection. Quiet meditation and deep worship are a prerequisite if you are to receive My words and comprehend My thoughts.

Some graces of the soul are gained in motion. Faith may be developed in action, endurance in the midst of storms and turmoil. Courage may come in the front lines of battle. But wisdom and understanding and revelation unfold as dew forms on the petals of a rose—in quietness.

Did not Jesus learn from His Father through the silences of lonely nights on the mountain? Shall I not teach you likewise? Will you, My child, set aside unto Me these hours for lonely vigil that I may have opportunity to minister to you?

Frances J. Roberts
Progress of Another Pilgrim

Hope in Purpose

"For I know the plans I have for you,"
declares the LORD, "plans to prosper
you and not to harm you, plans to
give you hope and a future."

JEREMIAH 29:11 NIV

We all need to have a sense of why we are here. We all need to know we were created for a purpose. We will never find fulfillment and happiness until we are doing the thing for which we were created. But God won't move us into the big things He has called us to unless we have been proven faithful in the small things He has given us. So if you are doing what you deem to be small things right now, rejoice! God's getting you ready for big things ahead.

Don't think for a moment that if you haven't moved into the purposes God has for you by now that it's too late. It is never too late. I did everything late. I didn't come to the Lord until I was twenty-eight. I got married late, had children late, and I didn't even start writing professionally until I was over forty. My whole ministry happened when I was in my forties and most of it in my fifties. Trust me, if you are still breathing, God has a purpose for you. He has something for you to do now.

Stormie Omartian
The Power of a Praying Woman

Fearfully and Wonderfully Made

For you created my inmost being; you
knit me together in my mother's womb.
I praise you because I am fearfully and
wonderfully made; your works are
wonderful, I know that full well.

PSALM 139:13–14 NIV

I do think God wants us to take reasonable care of our bodies. After all, it is the only living sacrifice we have to offer Him, and the scripture does say physical training is beneficial (Romans 12:1; 1 Corinthians 9:24–27; and 1 Timothy 4:8). But the obsessive pursuit of perfection is not reasonable—and it will never bring us the love we desire.

At the end of the day it's not beauty and physical fitness that we really want. What we really want is someone to love us. And we think that means we have to make ourselves lovable. But love isn't love if you have to earn it. Real love—God's love—is unconditional. He even loves women with cellulite. In fact, His Word says we are fearfully and wonderfully made, just the way we are. We don't need to change a thing to be lovable.

I think what God wanted to say to me—and what I was finally able to hear once He had my undivided attention—is that there are different kinds of love. And I was pursuing the wrong kind. Around this time, my children and I were sitting on the couch one evening. Tara looked up from my lap and said, "Mommy, you're the bestest pillow in the world." I don't think she could have said that with as much conviction to a thin-thighed mommy.

Donna Partow
This Isn't the Life I Signed Up For

Rich Promises

I will bless you [with abundant increase
of favors]. . .and you will be a blessing
[dispensing good to others].

GENESIS 12:2 AMP

The Bible is full of God's blessings for our lives,
full of positive words, promises granted to those
who choose to follow Him, who choose to believe in
His assurances. Hebrews 11:8 tells us that "by faith
Abraham obeyed when he was called to go out to the
place which he would receive as an inheritance" and
that "he went out, not knowing where he was going"
(NKJV). And when Abraham arrived at his destination, God met him there and gave him a brand-new
promise: "I will bless you. . .and you will be a blessing"
(Genesis 12:2 AMP). As sons and daughters of Abraham
(see Galatians 3:7), we share in this promise! We can
be filled with assurance that wherever we go, God will
bless us. He is even going before us, ready to greet us
with a word of encouragement when we get there.

Is your faith strong enough and your mind open
enough to make room for God's bounty of blessings?

Or is your faith too little, your mind too closed? Perhaps you feel you are undeserving. If so, plant the words of Hebrews 11:6 in your heart: "Without faith it is impossible to please and be satisfactory to Him. For whoever would come near to God must [necessarily] believe that God exists and that He is the rewarder of those who earnestly and diligently seek Him [out]" (AMP). Claim the promise of 1 John 5:14–15: "Now this is the confidence that we have in Him, that if we ask anything according to His will, He hears us. And if we know that He hears us, whatever we ask, we know that we have the petitions that we have asked of Him" (NKJV). It's not a matter of deserving but of firm faith, great expectation, and sincere seeking.

Donna K. Maltese
Power Prayers to Start Your Day

He Enjoys You

The LORD your God is in your midst,
a mighty one who will save;
he will rejoice over you with gladness;
he will quiet you by his love;
he will exult over you with loud singing.

ZEPHANIAH 3:17 ESV

Memory is a powerful part of each one of us. Perhaps you can see your father cheering you on in a sports event, or you remember your mother stroking your feverish forehead while you lay sick in bed. With those mental pictures comes a recollection of emotion—how good it felt to be cheered and encouraged—how comforting it was to be loved and attended.

Zephaniah's words remind us that God is our loving parent. Our mighty Savior offers us a personal relationship, loving and rejoicing over us, His children, glad that we live and move in Him. He is the Lord of the universe, and yet He will quiet our restless hearts and minds with His tender love. He delights in our lives and celebrates our union with Him. We can rest in His affirmation and love, no matter what circumstances surround us.

Leah Slawson
Daily Encouragement for Single Women

Hope in Song

"Hear, O kings; give ear, O rulers!
I—to the LORD, I will sing, I will sing
praise to the LORD, the God of Israel."

JUDGES 5:3 NASB

If you only knew, dear hesitating friends, what strength and gladness the Master gives when we loyally sing forth the honor of His name, you would not forego it! Oh, if you only knew the difficulties it saves! For when you sing "always and only for your King," you will not get much entangled by the King's enemies. Singing an out-and-out sacred song often clears one's path at a stroke as to many other things. If you only knew the rewards He gives, very often then and there, the recognition that you are one of the King's friends by some lonely and timid one; the openings which you quite naturally gain of speaking a word for Jesus to hearts which, without the song, would never have given you the chance! If you only knew the joy of believing that His sure promise, "My Word shall not return unto Me void" will be fulfilled as you sing that word for Him! If you only tasted the solemn happiness of knowing that you have indeed a royal audience, that the King Himself is listening as you sing! If you only knew, and why should you not know? Shall not the time past of your life suffice you for the miserable, double-hearted, calculating service? Let Him have the whole use of your voice at any cost, and see if He does not put many a totally unexpected new song into your mouth!

I am not writing all this to great and finished singers, but to everybody who can sing at all. Those who think they have only a very small talent are often most tempted not to trade with it for their Lord. Whether you have much or little natural voice, there is reason for its cultivation and room for its use. Place it at your Lord's disposal, and He will show you how to make the most of it for Him; for not seldom His multiplying power is brought to bear on a consecrated voice.

Frances Ridley Havergal
Kept for the Master's Use

Seeking to Please Jesus

Then the servant girl who kept the
door said to Peter, "You are not
also one of this Man's disciples,
are you?" He said, "I am not."

JOHN 18:17 NKJV

For three years Peter publicly followed Jesus. The disciple stood near the Master during the miracles, the messages, and all the good times. Everyone could see him sticking by Jesus.

But when Jesus came before the high priest, His life in danger, Peter caved in to fear and denied his Lord to a simple servant girl. Why would he care what a slave thought? Perhaps he feared that word of his presence would get back to the ruling priests.

Like Peter, we've caved in because of what others we barely knew thought of us. Instead of obeying the Lord we've loved, we've sought approval of both people who barely matter and those who could have some earthly authority over us. In a split second, love for the all-powerful Lord hardly seemed to matter.

Instead of allowing fear to rule our lives, we need

to steadfastly rest in Jesus' love. He who holds the entire world in His hands can direct our lives in the face of bad opinions from those who think ill of us. When we're faithful to Him, we hold firm to the One who really matters.

Lord, I want to hold on to You and please You only. Give me strength to do what I cannot do under my own power.

Pamela L. McQuade
Daily Wisdom for the Workplace

Jesus Is Coming!

"Therefore you also be ready,
for the Son of Man is coming
at an hour you do not expect."

MATTHEW 24:44 NKJV

Look at it from the non-Christian point of view: We Christians say the person we love most in all time and eternity will return to us, bypassing death and the grave and coming again in glory. This person isn't a sweetheart, spouse, or much-loved parent. As much as we're devoted to the folks we share earth with, we claim they cannot give us hope because they cannot conquer death.

This hope in Jesus seems silly to the world. Though we've never met Him face-to-face, we believe He still lives. Our hearts belong entirely to this unseen One. Without viewing Him in the flesh, we believe He will return. How can anyone understand such attitudes unless they, too, have met the Savior?

We tell them that the One we trust in said He's coming again. Do we completely rely on that seemingly impossible fact? Do we know He could come at any hour, any day? And are we ready for Him to appear? If we're ready, we're living every day as if we could see His face for the first time. Is this the unexpected hour?

Pamela McQuade
Daily Wisdom for the Workplace

Fruit for the Picking

Early in the morning, as Jesus was on his way back to the city, he was hungry. Seeing a fig tree by the road, he went up to it but found nothing on it except leaves. Then he said to it, "May you never bear fruit again!" Immediately the tree withered.

MATTHEW 21:18–19 NIV

Everything in nature is designed to grow, to produce fruit. Jesus cursed a fig tree once for giving the illusion of having fruit to offer. It was in full bloom but bore no figs. He commanded it to wither and die (Matthew 21:18–19). It was useless, taking up space and pretending to be something that it was not.

Some people are like this fig tree. They walk through life appearing to have a lot to offer, but up close, you find great pretenders. They bear no "fruit"—have nothing useful to give others—they're all show and no substance. A lack of productivity and the refusal to mature will stymie a life that is working—and it won't work for long.

God wants us moving forward, being productive,

maturing from the challenges we face. We then have "fruit" to share—the life lessons we pick up along the way. When we pass on these lessons, we empower others to grow and be fruitful as well. This is the cycle of life. We cross-pollinate!

Michelle McKinney Hammond
How to Make Life Work

Vision of Hope

Be stunned and amazed,
blind yourselves and be sightless;
be drunk, but not from wine,
stagger, but not from beer.

ISAIAH 29:9 NIV

It has always been my favorite theory that the blind can accomplish nearly everything that may be done by those who can see. Do not think that those who are deprived of physical vision are shut out from the best that earth has to offer her children. There are a few exceptions that instantly come to my mind. For example, through the medium of sight alone, does the astronomer mark the courses, the magnitudes and the varied motions of all the heavenly bodies; and only through the medium of the eye can the sculptor produce a beautiful statue from the rude and uncut marble. So, likewise, of the painter.

From attaining high rank in these fine arts, the blind of necessity, are debarred; but not so from poetry and music, in which the mind gives us a true image of the reality. Almost every lad at school is able to relate stray bits of legendary lore of ancient and modern artists who have been blind. Indeed, who can forget Euclid, the blind geometrician; or Homer, the blind bard; or Milton, the author?

A great many people fancy that the blind learn music only by ear, never by note; and yet a number of musical experts have told me that their blind pupils learn as proficiently as others by the latter method. It is truly wonderful—marvelous—to what a degree the memory can be trained, not only by those who rely upon it for most of their knowledge of the external world, but by all who wish to add to their general intellectual culture. But why should the blind be regarded as objects of pity? Darkness may indeed throw a shadow over the outer vision; but there is no cloud, however dark, that can keep the sunlight of hope from the trustful soul.

Fanny Crosby
Memories of Eighty Years

Above the Clouds

"I, even I, am he who comforts you."

ISAIAH 51:12 NIV

Every time I take off in an airplane on a gray, dreary, rainy day, I'm always amazed at how we can fly right up through the dark, wet clouds, so thick that we can't see one thing out the window, and then suddenly rise above it all and have the ability to see for miles. Up there the sky is sunny, clear, and blue. I keep forgetting that no matter how bad the weather gets, it's possible to rise above the storm to a place where everything is fine.

Our spiritual and emotional lives are much the same. When the dark clouds of trial, struggle, grief, or suffering roll in and settle on us so thick that we can barely see ahead of us, it's easy to forget there is a place of calm, light, clarity, and peace we can rise to. If we take God's hand in those difficult times, He will lift us up above our circumstances to the place of comfort, warmth, and safety He has for us.

One of my favorite names for the Holy Spirit is the

Comforter (John 14:26 KJV). Just as we don't have to beg the sun for light, we don't have to beg the Holy Spirit for comfort either. He is comfort.

Stormie Omartian
The Power of a Praying Woman

Water of Life

Come near to God and
he will come near to you.

JAMES 4:8 NIV

O My daughter, shall I speak unto thee as one whose voice is lost in the noise of crashing surf, or as one who calls in vain in the midst of a deep forest, where there is no ear to hear nor voice to respond? Will ye be as an instrument with broken strings from which the musician can bring forth no music?

Nay, I would have you to be as the waterfall whose sound is continuous, and as a great river whose flow is not interrupted. Ye shall not sing for a time and then be silent for a season. Ye shall not praise for a day, and then revert to the current topics of everyday life.

Ye shall never exhaust My supply. The more ye give, the more will be given unto thee. Ye are in a learning process. I have much to share with thee; yea, out of the abundance of My heart would I instruct thee. I would teach you truths of heavenly wisdom which ye cannot learn from the lips of man. I will instruct thee in the way that thou shalt go. From whom else can ye inquire?

I will bring My love and My life to thee. From whence have ye any such comfort and strength elsewhere? The more often ye come to Me to draw of this water of Life, the more shall thy life be enriched in wisdom— yes, but also in many other ways. Ye have need of My grace that ye may share My truth with a right spirit. Ye need to keep thy channel straight and clear, that My blessing be not hindered in flowing through thee, and that the waters may be kept pure.

Frances J. Roberts
Come Away My Beloved

Contagious Laughter

And Sarah said, "God has made me laugh,
and all who hear will laugh with me."

GENESIS 21:6 NKJV

Nothing brings more joy to our hearts than when God blesses our lives. Like Sarah, we may at first laugh with disbelief when God promises us our heart's desire. For some reason, we doubt that He can do what we deem impossible. Yet God asks us, as He did Sarah, "Is anything too hard for the LORD?" (Genesis 18:14 NKJV).

Then when the blessings shower down upon us, we overflow with joy. Everything seems bright and right with the world. With God, the impossible has become a reality. We bubble over with laughter, and when we laugh, the world laughs with us! It's contagious!

When Satan bombards us with lies—"God's not real"; "You'll never get that job"; "Mr. Right? He'll never come along"—it's time to look back at God's Word and remember Sarah. Imbed in your mind the truth that with God, nothing is impossible (see Matthew 19:26).

And then, in the midst of the storm, in the darkness of night, in the crux of the trial, laugh, letting the joy of God's truth be your strength.

Donna K. Maltese
Whispers of Wisdom for Busy Women

Getting Zinged

"Bless those who curse you,
pray for those who mistreat you."

LUKE 6:28 NIV

Let's be honest; we've all been zinged. You know, those comments that are said so sweetly that it isn't until you walk away that you realize you were insulted, like, "I love your hair; it looks like something from the forties." Yeah, I loved hearing that one.

As an individual who is blessed to breathe air, you're sure to have received a zinger. And as women, we've been blessed with long memories that allow us to relive those comments over and over again.

When the zingers come—and they will come—you have two choices. You can respond emotionally, leaving godly grace at the door, or you can respond in love—either by remaining silent or by gently responding to the comment. The choice is yours.

However, if you're listening to the Holy Spirit, you know that He won't let you get away with responding with a verbal assault. No, it's much better to respond in love. And the next time you see the "zingee," follow the advice found in Luke 6:28, and pray for God's blessing in her life. As you do, God promises that "your reward will be great" (Luke 6:35), and you will become more and more like Him.

Gena Maselli
Daily Wisdom for Working Women

I Am My Master's Treasure

"Look at the birds of the air, that they do not sow, nor reap nor gather into barns, and yet your heavenly Father feeds them. Are you not worth much more than they?"

MATTHEW 6:26 NASB

The opal is a beautiful stone, but when it lies in a jeweler's case, it's cold and lusterless, with no life in it. But let the jeweler pick it up in his hand and the warmth of his touch brings out the brilliant hues and colors. Likewise, when we hold the Lord at arm's length and refuse to let Him work in our lives, there is no brilliance, no color, no depth to living. But when we allow the touch of the Master's hand, His love warms us and we know we are jewels for His kingdom. Until then we are hidden treasures.

You may have seen the picture of the little boy saying, "I know I'm SOMEBODY. . .'cause GOD don't make no JUNK!" That little boy has a better understanding of God's love and forgiveness than many adult parents do. Their self-esteem has been destroyed because of something that's gone wrong in the family. Guilt has destroyed their self-esteem, and they feel worthless. I know that feeling—I felt it for eleven months without relief, and I still feel it occasionally when I momentarily forget I am very special to God.

Barbara Johnson
The Best of Barbara Johnson

Our New Name

You will be called by a new name
that the mouth of the LORD will bestow.

ISAIAH 62:2 NIV

The God of the Universe loves us passionately. In spite of this, we have thought of ourselves based on how we feel or others' expectations of us. But there is a truth that changes lives, transforms hearts and minds. It is a truth that sets us free from chains that have restrained us for years. We have been given a new identity, a true identity—an identity that Christ died to give us.

Regardless of past sins or ongoing struggles, God is taken with us. The Bible says that He has loved us with an everlasting love and cheers us along with His loving-kindness. He has clothed us with garments of salvation and arrayed us in robes of righteousness like a bride who adorns herself with jewels. As a groom rejoices over his bride, so God rejoices over us and declares us as lovely.

While on the cross, Jesus Christ took our sin and gave us His righteousness.

We have an identity in Him that cannot be stripped away by anyone or anything. We still make mistakes. But as we go to Him with repentant hearts, He forgives and cleanses us, and calls us restored.

We have been given names that we were never meant to answer to. We have named ourselves out of our own yearning to find a place to belong. But the good news is, Jesus has come to give us a new name. And it's time we start answering to it.

Jocelyn Hamsher
Circle of Friends

Rewiring My Buttons

Now that you have purified yourselves
by obeying the truth so that you have
sincere love for each other, love one
another deeply, from the heart.

1 PETER 1:22 NIV

Do you ever feel like you could be just a dandy Christian if it weren't for other people?

Sometimes I feel like I could shower love and goodwill all around me until someone goes and pushes my buttons. When conflict raises its ugly head, watch out! The un-Christian thoughts that sometimes run through my head are not glorifying to my Lord and Savior.

And yet God put me into a world where I have to interact with other people—even people who sometimes cause me to get a little grumpy, even downright mad. Jesus dealt with these kinds of people all the time. They were always trying to push His buttons and make Him say or do something wrong. The neat thing is that they never could. Jesus didn't have any buttons that made Him say or do mean things. He was perfect. I wish I were more like Him and didn't have those buttons. But, because I am a sinful creature, I do. And I need to rewire them so that when my buttons are pushed, I react with patience and love instead of frustration and anger, just like Jesus reacted. Surely I could follow the example of my Lord and Savior whom I claim to love and follow. Who, I know for a fact, puts up with some very annoying behaviors from me and constantly forgives me.

I think it's time to do some rewiring.

Janine Miller
Circle of Friends

The Lovely Will of God

Let God transform you into a new person
by changing the way you think. Then you
will learn to know God's will for you,
which is good and pleasing and perfect.

ROMANS 12:2 NLT

Formerly it had seemed to me that His will was the terrible instrument of His severity and that I must do all I could to avert its terrors from swooping down upon my devoted head. Now I saw that it was impossible for the will of unselfish love to be anything but good and kind.

It was not that life was to have no more trials, for this wise and loving will might see that trials were a necessary gift of love. Neither was it essential that we should be able to see the divine hand in every trial. Because He loves us with an unselfish and limitless love, He cannot fail to make the apparently hard or cruel or even wicked thing work together for our best good.

No matter who starts our trial, if God permits it to reach us, He has made the trial His own and will turn it for us into a chariot of love which will carry our souls to a place of blessing that we could not have reached in any other way.

God's will is the most lovely thing the universe contains for us, not because it always looks or seems the best, but because it cannot help being the best, since it is the will of infinite unselfishness and of infinite love.

Hannah Whitall Smith
The Unselfishness of God

Unmerited Love

God shows his love for us in that while
we were still sinners, Christ died for us.

ROMANS 5:8 ESV

The truth is, God does love us. Whether or not
we feel loved, regardless of what we have done
or where we have come from, He loves us with an
infinite, incomprehensible love.

God loves me—not because I have loved Him
since I was four years old, not because I seek to please
Him, not because I speak at conferences and write
books. He loves me—because He is love. His love for
me is not based on anything I have ever done or ever
could do for Him. It is not based on my performance.
I do not deserve His love and could never earn it.

The scripture says that when I was His enemy, He
loved me. You say, "How could you have been God's
enemy when you were a little girl?" According to the
Bible, from the moment I was born, I was ungodly,
a sinner, God's enemy, and deserving of His eternal
wrath (Romans 5:6–10). In spite of my alienation
from Him, He loved me and sent His Son to die for

me. He loved me in eternity past; He will love me for all eternity future. There is nothing I could do to make Him love me any less; there is nothing I could do to make Him love me any more.

Nancy Leigh DeMoss
Lies Women Believe and the Truth That Sets Them Free

God's Precious Riches

God will supply all your needs according to His riches in glory in Christ Jesus.

PHILIPPIANS 4:19 NASB

When the Bible writers describe our riches in Jesus Christ, they often use words starting with "un": joy unspeakable (see 1 Peter 1:8), unsearchable riches (see Ephesians 3:8), and unspeakable gifts (see 2 Corinthians 9:15). It seems as if they cannot find words to show the abundance the Lord gives us.

I think the reason is that the boundless resources of God's promises are celestial. They are earthly reproductions of heavenly riches in Jesus Christ, and they are ours under every circumstance.

All of His riches are for us—not to admire, but to take and keep. The antichrist is marching on and organizing his army over the whole world, but we stand on the Lord's side and may accept all His promises.

Too often we are like people who stand in front of the show window of a jewelry store. We admire the beautiful watches, rings, and bracelets, but we do not go in and pay the price in order to possess them. We just walk away! It is through Jesus that God's greatest and most precious promises have become available to us.

Corrie ten Boom
The End Battle

Walking in God-Confidence

If my people, who are called by my
name, will humble themselves and
pray and seek my face. . .then I will
hear from heaven, and I will forgive
their sin and will heal their land.

2 Chronicles 7:14 niv

Some people consider humility a weakness. Others
think humility means never talking about yourself or
always putting yourself and your accomplishments down.
Christians often confuse humility with low self-esteem,
believing we should not think of ourselves as worthy,
because Jesus Christ was the only perfect person.

But when we accept Christ as our Lord and Savior,
His life becomes ours. We are no longer slaves to
sin, but we own His righteousness. So we don't have
to go around thinking that we're scum. Since God
reconciled us to Himself through Jesus' sacrifice on
the cross, we can live each day with the confidence of
knowing we're forgiven.

Our Savior walked in total God-confidence—
knowing that His steps were planned—and He had

only to listen to His Father's heartbeat to know which way to go. He could withstand insults, persecutions, and dim-witted disciples because He knew who He was and where He was headed.

Today, humble yourself in front of God and ask His forgiveness for the ways you've sinned. Accept His forgiveness and live in total God-confidence, knowing that He has heard you. Then you'll be able to withstand the pressures life throws at you, because He is your life.

Dena Dyer

Daily Encouragement for Single Women

Hope in God's Keeping

You will be secure, because there
is hope; you will look about you
and take your rest in safety.

JOB 11:18 NIV

What is to be for Him? We talk sometimes as if, whatever else could be subdued unto Him, self could never be. But our true self is the new self, taken and won by the love of God, and kept by the power of God.

And kept for Him! Why should it be thought a thing incredible with you, when it is only the fulfilling of His own eternal purpose in creating us? "This people have I formed for Myself." Not ultimately only, but presently and continually; for he says, "Thou shalt abide for Me," and, "He that remaineth, even he shall before our God." Are you one of His people by faith in Jesus Christ? Then see what you are to Him. You, personally and individually, are part of the Lord's portion (Deuteronomy 32:9) and of His inheritance (1 Kings 8:53 and Ephesians 1:18). His portion and inheritance would not be complete without you. You are His peculiar treasure (Exodus 19:5); a special people (how warm, and loving, and natural that expression is!), "unto Himself" (Deuteronomy 7:6 KJV). Would you call it "keeping" if you had a special treasure, a darling little child, for instance, and let it run wild into all sorts of dangers all day long—sometimes at your side, and sometimes out in the street, with only the intention of fetching it safe home at night? If ye then, being evil, would know better and do better than that, how much more shall our Lord's keeping be true, and tender, and continual, and effectual, when He declares us to be His peculiar treasure, purchased (see 1 Peter 2:9) for Himself at such unknown cost!

Frances Ridley Havergal
Kept for the Master's Use

The Heart's Truth

Jesus asked, "You of little faith,
why are you talking among yourselves
about having no bread? Do you still not
understand? Don't you remember the
five loaves for the five thousand, and
how many basketfuls you gathered? . . .
How is it you don't understand that I
was not talking to you about bread?"

MATTHEW 16:8–11 NIV

Until the will and the affections are brought
under the authority of Christ, we have not
begun to understand, let alone to accept, His lordship. The cross, as it enters the love life, will reveal the
heart's truth. My heart, I knew, would be forever a
lonely hunter unless settled "where true joys are to be
found."

One morning I was reading the story of Jesus'
feeding of the five thousand. The disciples could find
only five loaves of bread and two fishes. "Let me have
them," said Jesus. He asked for all. He took them, said
the blessing, and broke them before He gave them
out. I remembered what a chapel speaker, Ruth Stull

of Peru, has said: "If my life is broken when given to Jesus, it is because pieces will feed a multitude, while a loaf will satisfy only a little lad."

Elisabeth Elliot
Passion and Purity

Focus and Balance

But more than anything else, put God's work first and do what he wants. Then the other things will be yours as well.

MATTHEW 6:33 CEV

I constantly struggle with my priorities. I think they are all in order, and then I find that in a very short time, I have to work on them again. Plus I am sure that I have attention deficit disorder. These disorders were not discovered when I was young, but I start five major projects all at one time, and my mind goes in ten directions at once, jumping from one thing to another so quickly that I can't even keep up. Consequently, I tend to become too busy very quickly.

Being too busy is enemy number one to my to-do list. I get talked into so many good things. One of the most difficult things for me is to say no to something or someone. Yet when I look at my list, whether mental or written, and examine it before the Lord, I often have to say no in order to be obedient to Him. He has given each of us the ability and freedom to say no; we just don't use it.

Thomas à Kempis reminds us that, just as it is often our duty to do what we don't particularly want to do, it is also our duty at times to leave undone what we want to do. Making and keeping our priorities in order and balanced takes a conscious effort and involves making conscious decisions.

Gigi Graham Tchividjian
A Quiet Knowing

Pressed, Yet Peaceful

Master, the multitude throng thee and
press thee. . . . And he said unto her,
Daughter, be of good comfort: thy faith
hath made thee whole; go in peace.

LUKE 8:45, 48 KJV

Many know that crushed feeling. I think our Lord must have thought of how often his followers would be "pressed out of measure, above strength," as one of them said, because of the throng of things, and because power had gone out of them; and so He allowed this lovely story to be told. Thronged, pressed, crushed, tired—for a man is tired when, in some special way, power has gone forth from him, and as He was man as well as God He must have been tired then—yet He was so peaceful that He could bring peace to the one who was fearing and trembling.

The more one ponders such a story, the more one sees in it, and the more one longs to live that life of victory over circumstances, the life which, though outwardly crowded and crushed, is yet overflowing with peace.

May the peace of our dear Lord fill every hour
with peace today.

Amy Carmichael
Edges of His Ways

A Courageous Queen

For momentary, light affliction is
producing for us an eternal weight
of glory far beyond all comparison.

2 CORINTHIANS 4:17 NASB

Katie was only eleven years old when the doctors removed her cancerous leg below the knee. She felt her young life was over.

"Who will ever want me?" she cried. "I'll never be able to walk or run again."

Katie did learn how to walk, and life returned to a new kind of normal, though she kept her prosthesis hidden from the world. But then God began nudging Katie to return to the hospital where she had her surgery to talk to other children facing similar ordeals. She put her fears aside and visited the cancer ward and showed a girl named Amanda her leg.

"Here, go ahead and touch it," she said. "It's okay." And Katie saw something flicker in Amanda's eyes. It was hope. . . .

Katie decided it was time to stop hiding her leg from the world, and she did it in a big way. She entered the Miss University of Central Arkansas pageant! She participated in the talent, evening gown, and interview competitions. But she won the heart of the crowd when she proudly walked down the catwalk during the bathing suit competition. . . . I daresay there was never a more precious moment than when Katie Signaigo was crowned Miss UCA.

No, Katie's life was not over when the doctors removed her leg to save her. It was the beginning of an exciting journey filled with many extraordinary moments with God.

Sharon Jaynes
Extraordinary Moments with God

An Exhortation

Then David continued, "Be strong
and courageous, and do the work.
Don't be afraid or discouraged, for
the LORD God, my God, is with you.
He will not fail you or forsake you."

1 CHRONICLES 28:20 NLT

In 1 Chronicles 28:20, King David has just given his son Solomon and the people of Israel detailed instructions for building the Lord's temple. Can you imagine how awed and overwhelmed the people felt as they heard the plans for the temple's design? First Kings 5 and 6 tell us that it took tens of thousands of skilled workmen seven years to complete the temple! No wonder David exhorted his people to be strong and courageous! No wonder he urged them to resist discouragement and fear!

God knew His people could complete the undertaking He had set before them, but He also knew they would be overwhelmed by the enormity of the task. Perhaps you, too, are feeling disheartened by the sheer size of your responsibilities. Maybe you feel like giving up. David's words still offer us encouragement in the face of the seemingly insurmountable: Be strong and courageous! Do the work! Don't be afraid or discouraged by the size of the task. The Lord God is with you, and He will not fail you or forsake you!

Mandy Nydegger
Whispers of Wisdom for Busy Women

Knowing God Brings Hope

Shout for joy to the LORD, all the
earth. Worship the LORD with gladness;
come before him with joyful songs.
Know that the LORD is God. It is he
who made us, and we are his; we are
his people, the sheep of his pasture.

PSALM 100:1–3 NIV

In the middle of this psalm of thanksgiving comes
this little nugget of spiritual gold, "Know that the
Lord is God." It may seem random, but when we look
closer we find it isn't out of place at all.

When we know who God is, it lays a foundation
upon which we can build our lives. We can shout and
sing in His presence because we know who we are
praising and why. Our worship has a focus, an object
of adoration—a holy and righteous God. He is the
One who made us and we belong to Him. That is
where our thanksgiving and praise come from!

He is good. He pours out mercy and grace in an
unending stream. His truth endures generation after
generation. Knowing all these things—who God is,

what He has done, and that He has chosen us and will take care of us—gives us a bedrock of faith to stand upon when circumstances overwhelm us. We are not shaken, we are not moved—because we know.

Missy Horsfall
Circle of Friends

You're Not Too Old

"For I know the plans I have for you,"
says the LORD. "They are plans for
good and not for disaster, to give
you a future and a hope."

JEREMIAH 29:11 NLT

Do you sometimes feel like the best part of your life is already over? That can be the cause of intense unhappiness and dissatisfaction. In fact, several studies have revealed that the older a person gets, the more likely it is that that person will become depressed. It seems old age and depression go hand in hand.

But they don't have to!

No matter what your age, you are not too old to fulfill the plans God has for your life.

Did you know that Grandma Moses started painting at age seventy-six? Without any art classes or special training, she painted simple, realistic pictures of rural settings—paintings of historic importance.

So what dreams has God placed inside you? Is it to write a book? To start your own business? What's holding you back? In Jeremiah 29:11, God said He had good plans for His people. Don't you think He has a good plan for you?

If you feel like you're too old, ask God to change your perception of yourself. He wants you to realize your dreams because He's the One who put them there.

Jesus came to give you a full life. But you have to want it, too! Spend some time today meditating on your dreams—even those you have let go of—and commit to praying over them until they are realized. That faithfulness in itself will bring happiness and hope.

Michelle Medlock Adams
Secrets of Happiness

Always a Bright Side

"I will forget my complaint,
I will change my expression, and smile."

JOB 9:27 NIV

There is a real art in smiling. Some people smile, or grin, all the time, and it becomes monotonous to those who look at them. These grinning people never seem to think who or what their smile is for. It is as if their mouths were made in that form. Other people have the kind of smile upon their faces that suggests sarcasm. But there are still others, and I have met [women] who had mastered the art, whose smiles are tear chasers. There is something so understanding in their glance and smile that they make you feel that they care for you and want you to be happy. Sometimes when I have been discouraged or depressed by trials all my own, a bright, hopeful smile from someone has cheered me amazingly. In fact, we are very much dependent upon each other for courage and happiness. Then let us be dispensers of joy as we go through life, smiling and glad. If I am in trouble, having acted foolishly in something or other, then I do not appreciate the grinning smile. I would rather the face that looked into mine would express a little understanding and feeling for my trouble or that it would not notice my foolishness at all; when I find a friend who can meet me this way, then that friend becomes a real comfort and joy to me.

Smiles and gladness are like sweet peas in that the more you gather and give away, the more you have. Leave your sweet peas on the vines, and the flowers are soon gone, but gather them closely each day, and they will blossom the more and last the summer through. So save your smiles for special occasions, when there are joys abroad, and you will pretty nearly run out of them altogether, but give them out at every opportunity, and the joy vines of your heart will thrive and grow. Live in the sunshine. Look on the bright side, for always there is a bright side.

Mabel Hale
Beautiful Girlhood

Doing Good Work

For we are his workmanship,
created in Christ Jesus unto good
works, which God hath before
ordained that we should walk in them.

EPHESIANS 2:10 KJV

When we create something, it feels good to know we've done a good job. As we put the final touches on a report, a letter, or whatever widgets we make on the job, gladness fills us, not just that we've finished the job, but that we've done it well.

God enjoys creating things, too—like people. Imagine how He felt when He finished creating you. Did He smile, knowing He'd finished a masterpiece? Could He trust that here was a person who would do good works for Him out of deep love?

We may make a widget and never see it again. It becomes part of a car, building, or computer. A report or letter gets filed away, and few see it after the fact. But that's not so with God; He sees us every day of our lives and watches us fondly as we do the good works He prepared for us to accomplish. When that work is finished, He calls us home because He made us and wants to share eternity with us.

Is the work you're doing today something that will make the Creator proud?

Lord, thank You for making me to do good things that make You proud. Help me do those things today.

Pamela L. McQuade
Daily Wisdom for the Workplace

Hope in Surrender

I appeal to you therefore, brothers, by the mercies of God, to present your bodies as a living sacrifice, holy and acceptable to God, which is your spiritual worship.

ROMANS 12:1 ESV

There is no other way for you but to surrender utterly and to cast all your care on the Lord, and leave it there. You must not think of it or brood over it, but must dismiss it from your mind altogether, except whatever degree is necessary for proper self-care. But if your worst fears are confirmed, then you must bow your neck to the yoke and must accept your life as the very best thing that could have come to you.

You can only conquer your trial by submitting to it. But if you will submit, it will become your joy and crown of rejoicing. Lay yourself as a living sacrifice upon God's altar. Say "Yes" to Him about it all. "Yes, Lord, Yes. Your will, not mine. Your good and perfect will! I am content to suffer; I am content to be laid aside, if it is Your sweet will."

I'm sure that you must not always be looking

ahead. I am sure you must live just one day at a time, taking no thought of any kind for tomorrow. It is a glorious chance for you to abandon yourself unreservedly to the love and will of your Lord. And I believe if you will do this, it will be the doorway for you into a far deeper relationship with the Lord than you have ever known yet.

Hannah Whitall Smith
The Christian's Secret of a Holy Life

When We Need Help

"My sheep listen to my voice; I know
them, and they follow me. I give them
eternal life, and they shall never perish;
no one will snatch them out of my hand."

JOHN 10:27–28 NIV

As a college student I worried much about whether I would fail to follow the Shepherd, would be deaf to His call. I thought it such a bewildering matter.

It is not a worry anymore. Experience has taught me that the Shepherd is far more willing to show His sheep the path than the sheep are to follow. He is endlessly merciful, patient, tender, and loving. If we, His stupid and wayward sheep, really want to be led, we will without fail be led. Of that I am sure.

When we need help, we wish we knew somebody who was wise enough to tell us what to do, reachable when we need him, and even able to help us. God is. Omniscient, omnipresent, omnipotent—everything we need. The issue is confidence in the Shepherd Himself, a confidence so complete that we offer ourselves

without any reservation whatsoever and determine to
do what He says.

Elisabeth Elliot
Keep a Quiet Heart

Moses Is in Glory

And behold, two men were talking with
Him; and they were Moses and Elijah,
who, appearing in glory, were speaking
of His departure which He was about
to accomplish at Jerusalem.

LUKE 9:30–31 NASB

In case you've been feeling sorry for Moses who
never got to enter the Promised Land, just look at
what God had in store for him. These verses tell us
that Moses and Elijah appeared in glory. But what does
that really mean?

We are not now what we will become. For whether
we die or are taken up by what is referred to as the
Rapture, the Lord will someday allow this "earth suit"
of ours to fall away and issue us our "eternity suit."

"For if we believe that Jesus died and rose again,
even so God will bring with Him those who have fallen
asleep in Jesus. . . . For the Lord Himself will descend
from heaven with a shout, with the voice of the arch-
angel and with the trumpet of God, and the dead in
Christ will rise first. Then we who are alive and remain

will be caught up together with them in the clouds to meet the Lord in the air, and so we shall always be with the Lord" (1 Thessalonians 4:14, 16–17 NASB).

That day on top of the mountain, at Jesus' Transfiguration, the apostles witnessed Christ's glory and saw Moses and Elijah. And God spoke from the cloud which encompassed them saying, " 'This is my Son, whom I have chosen; listen to him' " (Luke 9:35 NIV).

In spite of your life, are you assured of your salvation?

Carol L. Fitzpatrick
Daily Wisdom for Women

Worship and Rest

RETURN TO YOUR REST, MY SOUL,
FOR THE LORD HAS BEEN GOOD TO YOU.

PSALM 116:7 NIV

I can't do it!" I cried to God in prayer shortly after Michael and I were married. "I can't handle the dishes—I can't handle the house—I can't handle my work—I can't handle the loneliness of being the wife of someone who works all the time—I can't deal with my own emotional ups and downs, let alone his! I can't do any of it, God, not any of it!"

I wept before the Lord with a mixture of frustration and guilt over the fact that I was feeling this way about my husband, my home, and my life. God had rescued me from the pit of hell and death just three years before and had given me a hope and a future. How could I—who knew what it was to be hungry and poor and feel there was no love or purpose in life—tell God I couldn't handle these answers to my own prayers?

Fortunately, the Lord did not strike me with lightning; He waited quietly until I was finished and then softly reminded me, *You are trying to do everything in your own strength.* As I sat there in my discouragement, I sensed the Holy Spirit speaking to my heart, saying simply, *All you have to do is worship Me in the midst of what you are facing, and I will do the rest.*

"Oh, thank You, Lord," I prayed through my tears. "I think I can at least handle doing that much."

Stormie Omartian
Finding Peace for Your Heart

Hope in His Plan

"Write down the revelation and make it plain on tablets so that a herald may run with it. For the revelation awaits an appointed time; it speaks of the end and will not prove false. Though it linger, wait for it; it will certainly come and will not delay."

HABAKKUK 2:2–3 NIV

Deborah is one of my heroes. At a time when the nation of Israel had strayed far from the worship of Jehovah and had been taken into captivity by the Canaanites, God raised up Deborah as a prophet and judge over the nation. Over the period of her rule, the Israelites gained their freedom as this courageous woman made wise decisions and led them into battle. What was the result? The entire land had peace for forty years. Deborah fulfilled her destiny because she followed God with faith and confidence.

We are all needed to make a holy difference in this world. In fact, God has chosen us to do just that (see John 15:16). God asks you and me to be outrageously convinced that the purpose of our time here on earth is truly significant. . .so convinced that we will not give up the pursuit of the spiritual dreams He has placed in our hearts.

If God is giving you a dream for your life, write the vision down. Describe it. You'll never do what you cannot visualize. Then let God calculate the route and the timing. When He says to move, step out by faith and continue until you reach your destination. He will fulfill the plans He has for you! Trust Him.

Joyce Strong
Author, Speaker

Omnipresent God

If I rise on the wings of the dawn,
if I settle on the far side of the sea,
even there your hand will guide me,
your right hand will hold me fast.

PSALM 139:9–10 NIV

Have you ever moved when it wasn't your choice? Maybe it was a job transfer. Or maybe finances required you to downsize from a house to an apartment. It may have been an adjustment to move out on your own after living with roommates. Perhaps you were needed back in your hometown to care for a sick relative. No matter the reason, a move is always somewhat unsettling.

Do you remember as a child when your family went to your grandparents' home for Christmas? Maybe you panicked at the thought of spending the night away from home on Christmas Eve. What if Santa didn't know where you were?

Think of how unsettling it was to lose a tooth while on vacation. Did the tooth fairy make visits to hotels? How would she ever locate the correct room number in order to deposit the dollar for the tooth under your pillow? Yet Santa and the tooth fairy always showed up! Amazingly, they knew right where you were.

So does God! He is omnipresent, always present everywhere. Our human minds cannot conceive it, but it is true. Wherever you live or travel, whatever unfamiliar place you find yourself in, remember God is there with you to guide you and to hold you tight.

Emily Biggers
Daily Encouragement for Single Women

Transforming Trust

Those who know your name trust
in you, for you, LORD, have never
forsaken those who seek you.

PSALM 9:10 NIV

As we look at the life of Christ and listen to His
words, we can hear God saying, "I am rest for the
weary; I am peace for the storm-tossed; I am strength
for the strengthless; I am wisdom for the foolish; I am
righteousness for the sinful; I am all that the neediest soul
on earth can want; I am exceeding abundantly, beyond all
you can ask or think, of blessing, and help, and care."

It is a piece of magnificent good news declared to
you in the Bible; and you only need do with it exactly
what you do when any earthly good news is told you by
a reliable earthly source. If the speaker is trustworthy,
you believe what he says and act in accordance. And you
must do the same here. If Christ is trustworthy when
He tells you that He is the manifestation of God, you
must believe what He says, and act accordingly. You must
take your stand on His trustworthiness. You must say
to yourself, and to your friends if need be, "I am going

to believe what Christ says about God. No matter what the seemings may be, nor what my own thoughts and feelings are, nor what anybody else may say, I know that what Christ says about God must be true, for He knew, and nobody else does, and I am going to believe Him right straight through, come what may. He says that He was one with God, so all that He was God is, and I will never be frightened of God anymore. I will never again let myself think of Him as a stern Lawgiver who is angry with me because of my sins, nor as a hard Taskmaster who demands from me impossible tasks, nor as a far-off unapproachable Deity who is wrapped up in His own glory and is indifferent to my sorrows and my fears. All such ideas of God have become impossible, now that I know that Christ was the true manifestation of God."

If we will take our stand on this one fact, that Christ and God are one, with an intelligent comprehension of what it involves, and will refuse definitely and unwaveringly to cherish any thought of God that is at variance with what Christ has revealed, life will be transformed for us.

Hannah Whitall Smith
The God of All Comfort

Love Is a Decision

"And now, Israel, what does the
LORD your God require of you?
He requires only that you fear the
LORD your God, and live in a way
that pleases him, and love him and
serve him with all your heart and soul."

DEUTERONOMY 10:12 NLT

Wouldn't it be great if we could require someone to love us? "But," I can hear you say, "how
can you require love? Love is a feeling—you can't
require someone to have a certain feeling!"

If love were a feeling, I would agree. But feelings are
only a part of love—and a very unreliable part at that.

The love God requires from us for Himself and for
each other is the highest form of love—*agape* love—
love like His. It is a love of the head rather than a love
of the heart. A love that determines to be concerned,
first and foremost, for the loved ones' well-being in
every dimension of their lives—whatever the cost to
ourselves and irrespective of their reaction.

So how can we know that we love God? By being

obedient. Jesus said, "Those who accept my commandments and obey them are the ones who love me" (John 14:21 NLT). This verse relieves my anxiety, as I've always worried that I wasn't loving God enough. My fears were based on my erratic feelings toward Him. These words of the Lord take the whole thing out of the realm of feelings and into the realm of doing. Now *that* I can handle! And what can I do to show God I love him? I can *do* for others. This is what He requires.

Jill Briscoe

The One Year Book of Devotions for Women

Beauty Instead of Ashes

To bestow on them a crown of beauty instead of ashes, the oil of joy instead of mourning, and a garment of praise instead of a spirit of despair. They will be called oaks of righteousness, a planting of the LORD for the display of his splendor.

ISAIAH 61:3 NIV

God is able to give comfort just when we need it. The past couple of days have been extremely difficult for me because it is the anniversary of the death of my seventeen-year-old daughter.

The beautiful part of the entire situation is that Liz is already in her eternity. She is walking those streets of gold, in total awe of our God! The comforting part is the total and complete miracle that God gave to us—His continuous presence and grace in our lives. He has truly turned our mourning to gladness.

The tears shed have served to cleanse our hearts, and allowed us to relieve the sorrow we felt. The best thing that there is about those tears is that God holds all of our tears in a bottle (Psalm 56:8). A few weeks ago, I began praying about these days and was reminded of that scripture about God saving my tears. I asked the Lord just what His plans are for all of the tears that He holds for all of His people. God spoke to my heart and reminded me of yet another scripture, where Jesus performed His first miracle. He turned the water into wine at the wedding at Cana (John 2:1–11).

I wonder. . .

Becki Reiser
Circle of Friends

Speak, Lord

Then call thou,
and I will answer.

JOB 13:22 KJV

What about the last time we knelt in prayer? Surely He had more to say to us than we had to say to Him, and yet we never waited a moment to see! We did not give Him opportunity for His gracious response. We rushed away from our King's presence as soon as we had said our say, and vaguely expected Him to send His answers after us somehow and sometime, but not there and then. What wonder if they have not yet reached us! The only wonder is that He ever speaks at all when we act thus. If Mary had talked to the Lord Jesus all the time she sat at His feet, she would not have "heard His word." But is not this pretty much what we have done?

Not that we should pray less, but listen more. And the more we listen, the more we shall want to say afterward. But we may miss the sweetest whispers of His love by not saying, "Speak, Lord," and not hushing ourselves to "hear what God the Lord will speak." We cannot hear His still, small voice during a torrent of noisy and impatient and hurried petition.

Frances Ridley Havergal
Daily Thoughts for the King's Children

Hope in His Presence

Then Jesus went to work on his disciples.
"Anyone who intends to come with me has
to let me lead. You're not in the driver's
seat; I am. Don't run from suffering;
embrace it. Follow me and I'll show you how."

MATTHEW 16:24 MSG

My little one, come close to Me. I have consolations for your soul that surpass your sharpest grief. I have walked through the deepest waters, and I am with you as you experience your baptism of sorrow. It is the path that leads to the gate of glory, and the Father waits to greet you there. It is not heaven of which I speak. It is a blessedness of spirit which is given to those who have passed through tribulations, have washed their robes, and have set their feet on the high road of absolute surrender. From this place there is no turning back. Having passed this point, there is no way to retreat.

Nothing whatever that may be demanded daunts the totally committed. It is the Father's good pleasure to give you the kingdom. Boundless is His love, and with great tenderness, He woos you into a place of favoritism. It may cost you all, but you cannot fathom what He has in store for you.

Hold fast to His hand. He will not lead anywhere except He be present all the time and all the way. Blessed fellowship and holy comfort!

Frances J. Roberts
On the Highroad of Surrender

Encourage and Strengthen Yourself

David was greatly distressed, for the
men spoke of stoning him because the
souls of them all were bitterly grieved,
each man for his sons and daughters.
But David encouraged and strengthened
himself in the Lord his God.

I SAMUEL 30:6 AMP

We all need people in our lives who encourage and strengthen us. But what about those times when even our most trusted friends are nowhere to be found? Has that ever happened to you? It happened to David. At one of the lowest moments of his life, when his wife and children had been kidnapped, no human being could comfort him because they all had "their own stuff" to deal with.

Fortunately, David had learned something all of us must learn: how to encourage and strengthen himself. We also need to take proactive steps to strengthen ourselves. You can't always rely on someone else. As motivational speaker Jim Rohn put it, "You can't hire someone else to do your push-ups for you."

One thing I do to encourage and strengthen myself is constantly listen to good Bible teaching—in my car, in my bathroom as I get dressed in the morning, in my kitchen while I'm preparing meals or cleaning up. . . . Of course listening to great Bible teachers is not a substitute for spending time in the Word of God.

Affirmation: I encourage and strengthen myself in the Lord.

Donna Partow
Becoming the Woman God Wants Me to Be

Hope in Dependence

> "Then the glory of the LORD will
> be revealed, and all flesh will
> see it together; for the mouth
> of the LORD has spoken."

ISAIAH 40:5 NASB

The Christian life is full of paradoxes, like this one: Only when we are totally dependent on our Redeemer are we truly free!

Carefully woven throughout chapters forty to sixty-six of Isaiah are specific portraits of Christ, presented by the names He called Himself throughout His ministry on earth. "Like a shepherd He will tend His flock, in His arm He will gather the lambs and carry them in His bosom; He will gently lead the nursing ewes" (Isaiah 40:11 NASB).

Then we will see Him as the Counselor. "Who has directed the Spirit of the LORD, or as His counselor has informed Him?" (Isaiah 40:13 NASB)

We can know Him as Creator. "Do you not know? Have you not heard? The Everlasting God, the LORD, the Creator of the ends of the earth does not become

weary or tired. His understanding is inscrutable"
(Isaiah 40:28 NASB).

Jesus is the First and the Last. "Who has performed and accomplished it, calling forth the genera-
tions from the beginning? 'I, the LORD, am the first,
and with the last. I am He' " (Isaiah 41:4 NASB). Christ
clarifies this further in Revelation 1:8: " 'I am the
Alpha and the Omega,' says the Lord God, 'who is and
who was and who is to come, the Almighty' " (NASB).

Carol L. Fitzpatrick
Daily Wisdom for Women

Available 24-7

I call on you, my God, for you
will answer me; turn your ear
to me and hear my prayer.

PSALM 17:6 NIV

No one is available to take your call at this time, so leave a message and we will return your call—or not—if we feel like it. . .and only between the hours of 4:00 and 4:30 p.m. Thank you for calling. Have a super day!

We've all felt the frustration of that black hole called voice mail. It is rare to reach a real, honest-to-goodness, breathing human being the first time we dial a telephone number.

Fortunately, our God is always available. He can be reached at any hour of the day or night and every day of the year—including weekends and holidays! When we pray, we don't have to worry about disconnections, hang-ups, or poor reception. We will never be put on hold or our prayers diverted to another department. The Bible assures us that God is eager to hear our petitions and that He welcomes our prayers of thanksgiving. The psalmist David wrote of God's response to those who put their trust in Him: "He will call on me, and I will answer him" (Psalm 91:15 NIV). David had great confidence that God would hear his prayers. And we can, too!

Austine Keller

Whispers of Wisdom for Busy Women

Hopeful Trust

Those who trust in the LORD are
like Mount Zion, which cannot
be shaken but endures forever.

PSALM 125:1 NIV

Does your job seem secure? Or are you constantly
listening to gossip at the watercooler or Coke
machine to discover the latest dirt about the corporate
finances? Are things looking up for your company, or
are they looking mighty grim?

Most of us expect our companies to provide
security. We all want good, secure jobs. But when a
company starts looking precarious, we worry about
the future and may even start looking for another
"good, secure job."

Our incomes keep us alive, so of course job security concerns us. We want to pay the rent and grocery
bills and can't do it if we don't work. But when we
place all our trust in companies, we'll experience
disappointment. CEOs can't predict the financial
future, hard as they try. Managers can't be certain our
positions won't be axed in a corporate downsize.

But when we look to God for security, we will never be shaken. He knows the future. He foresees what jobs we need, long before we find them. Even if we lose our jobs unexpectedly, He helps us pay the rent and feed the kids.

Today, are you trusting in a short-term business or an eternal Father?

Pamela McQuade
Daily Wisdom for the Workplace

He Loves Me!

Behold, what manner of love the
Father hath bestowed upon us, that
we should be called the sons of God.

1 JOHN 3:1 KJV

P oor child!" he said in a low voice, as if to himself.
"Poor, heartsick, tired child that cannot see what I
can see, that its Father's loving arms are all about it!"

I stopped crying, to strain my ears to listen. He
went on.

"Katy, all that you say may be true. I daresay it is.
But God loves you. He loves you."

"He loves me," I repeated to myself. "He loves
me. Oh, Dr. Cabot, if I could believe that! If I could
believe that, after all the promises I have broken, all
the foolish, wrong things I have done, and shall always
be doing, God perhaps still loves me!"

"You may be sure of it," he said solemnly. "I, His
minister, bring the Gospel to you today. Go home and
say over and over to yourself, 'I am a wayward, foolish
child. But He loves me! I have disobeyed and grieved
Him ten thousand times. But He loves me! I have lost

faith in some of my dearest friends and am very desolate. But He loves me! I do not love Him; I am even angry with Him. But He loves me!' "

Elizabeth Prentiss
Stepping Heavenward

The Dream List

Write the vision, and make
it plain upon tables, that he
may run that readeth it.

HABAKKUK 2:2 KJV

Years ago, I made a list of things I wanted to do
in my lifetime. It included things like sailing
around the world, attending the Olympics, going on a
cruise, and traveling Europe by train with my husband. I haven't accomplished all of them, and some I
no longer have an interest in doing, like skydiving or
hang gliding. (Those urges passed with the big hair
of the 1980s.) Still, it's fun to review the list and see
how many I've accomplished, which ones I no longer
want to do, and others that are yet to be done. And of
course, there are always new ones to add.

Writing down a vision—whether personal or
professional—is a great way to keep your dreams in
front of you. And as time passes, it's a great encouragement. During those times when you feel like
you're going nowhere, your list can remind you of all

that you've accomplished. Then you can thank God for giving you the desires of your heart, because He is the Author and Finisher of your life.

Gena Maselli
Daily Wisdom for Working Women

Giver of Good Things

For the LORD God is a sun and shield;
The LORD will give grace and glory;
No good thing will He withhold
From those who walk uprightly.

PSALM 84:11 NKJV

Worry is such a useless practice, like spinning wheels on a vehicle that takes you nowhere. And yet we women are notorious for it. The Bible advises us to let each day take care of itself. We are promised that God will provide for us.

Psalm 84:11 says that God is not a withholder of good things from His children. He knows us. He created us and put in us our own unique dreams, preferences, and hopes. When you begin to worry, read this verse. Put it on your bulletin board at work and your bathroom mirror at home. Read it aloud each time that worry begins to creep in.

Your heavenly Father is not "the big man upstairs" looking down upon you and laughing at the unfulfilled desires in your life. He wants to give you good things. Often His timing is different than ours, but His plan is always to bless and never to harm us. Look for the blessings in each day, and keep bringing your desires before the Lord in expectation.

Emily Biggers
Daily Encouragement for Single Women

Hope in Battle

"For the battle is not yours, but God's. . . .
You will not have to fight this battle.
Take up your positions; stand firm and see
the deliverance the LORD will give you."

2 CHRONICLES 20:15, 17 NIV

I remember once, as my two-year-old son was running to me, he tripped over himself and fell. He hopped up and said, "Oops, I dropped myself." He didn't get discouraged in his efforts to walk; he accepted this as par for the course for someone his age. He didn't compare himself to me, but on occasion, he did ask me to help him along.

Each time I "dropped myself" spiritually, the devil left his calling card of discouragement. I was measuring my spiritual growth and progress by the beautiful Christian role models around me. I was becoming more and more despondent because I couldn't measure up, instead of simply accepting and acknowledging my limitations, as my little son had done, and asking for His help, which He would have lovingly and readily given.

I began to wake up to the realization that if I

continued to try to live victoriously in my own strength, I could expect nothing but failure and discouragement. I began to see that I was expecting perfection. I was expecting more of myself than the Lord was expecting of me! I was trying to win the battles alone and was disappointed with myself when I lost. But the Lord doesn't expect us to fight alone. He says that He will go with us and fight for us.

Gigi Graham Tchividjian
A Quiet Knowing

A Place in the World

The Spirit of God has made me;
the breath of the Almighty gives me life.

JOB 33:4 NIV

A poor little blind girl, without influential friends, could have as many ambitions as anyone; but how was she to achieve them? What was there for her? The great world that could see was rushing past me day by day, and sweeping on toward the goal of its necessities and desires, while I was left stranded by the wayside. "Oh, you cannot do this—because you are blind, you know; you can never go there, because it would not be worthwhile: you could not see anything if you did, you know"—these and other things were often said to me, in reply to my many and eager questionings.

Often, when such circumstances as this made me very blue and depressed, I would creep off alone, kneel down, and ask God if, though blind, I was not one of His children—if in all His great world He had not some little place for me. And it often seemed that I could hear Him say, "Do not be discouraged, little girl; you shall someday be happy and useful, even in your blindness." And I would go back among my associates, cheered and encouraged and feeling that it would not be very long before my life would be full of activity and usefulness.

Fanny Crosby
Memories of Eighty Years

Choreography of Hope

My own hand laid the foundations
of the earth, and my right hand spread
out the heavens; when I summon them,
they all stand up together.

ISAIAH 48:13 NIV

Hardly a day goes by without my receiving a letter, a phone call, or a visit from someone in trouble. Almost always the question comes, in one form or another, *Why does God do this to me?*

When I am tempted to ask that same question, it loses its power when I remember that this Lord, into whose strong hands I long ago committed my life, is engineering a universe of unimaginable proportions and complexity. How could I possibly understand all that He must have taken into consideration as He deals with it and with me, a single individual! He has given us countless assurances that we cannot get lost in the shuffle. He choreographs the "molecular dance" which goes on every second of every minute of every day in every cell in the universe. For the record, one cell has about 200 trillion molecules. He makes note of the smallest seed and the tiniest sparrow. He is not too busy to keep records even of my falling hair.

Yet in our darkness we suppose He has overlooked us. He hasn't.

Elisabeth Elliot
Keep a Quiet Heart

He Wants to Hold Your Hand

"I will lead the blind by ways they have not known, along unfamiliar paths I will guide them; I will turn the darkness into light before them and make the rough places smooth. These are the things I will do; I will not forsake them."

ISAIAH 42:16 NIV

About fifteen years ago I called my mom while gulping back sobs and told her I felt like my life was falling apart. I was in the middle of a difficult job change, a good friend had been killed in a car accident, and I'd just found out that another friend was having an affair. I was disillusioned and depressed and said I could no longer see the proverbial light at the end of the tunnel.

Mom listened to me for a long time and then told me that I should start reading the book of Isaiah. She said he had a lot to say about dark, desperate places. I must admit I wasn't initially enthused or encouraged by her advice. I didn't want her to tell me to study some ancient prophet—I wanted her to FedEx a plane ticket to a tropical island!

But when I finally shut down my pity party and perused Isaiah, I discovered that mushrooms aren't the only things that grow in the dark. So does faith.

Reading this Old Testament prophecy didn't make the clouds in my life immediately vanish. It simply reminded me to pause and pray, to be still and listen for divine directions, and to quit whining and let God lead me.

Lisa Harper
What the Bible Is All About for Women

Hope of Freedom

Therefore, there is now no condemnation for those who are in Christ Jesus,
because through Christ Jesus the law of
the Spirit who gives life has set you free
from the law of sin and death.

ROMANS 8:1–2 NIV

As I sat across from this young mother, listening to
her story, my heart broke. The hand that life had
dealt her, poor choices, lack of family support, and
more contributed to the reason I was looking at her
through a thick pane of glass. She was in jail, weeping for the children she left behind, uncertain of her
future and feeling extremely alone.

Many of us are just like her. No, we may not have
broken the law, but we live in our own prison of sorts.
Emotionally, we chain ourselves to wrong thinking,
believing lies of who we are. We are shackled by loom-
ing guilt or shame that keeps us from moving forward
and embracing the plans God has for us. We have
locked our hearts behind a wall of protection so as not
to get hurt by others again. Some of us have never

invited Jesus into our lives while others of us who have, haven't followed Him. Whatever the situation, there are many of us who have experienced bondage.

There is hope for all of us. No matter what we have done or how long we have been behind "bars," Jesus is inviting us to take His hand and follow Him. Because of Jesus Christ, we don't have to live in condemnation any longer. Jesus has unlocked the prison door and set us free.

Jocelyn Hamsher
Circle of Friends

Mirror, Mirror

I praise you because of the
wonderful way you created me.
Everything you do is marvelous!

PSALM 139:14 CEV

How do you see yourself? Do you have a negative perception? When you look in the mirror, do you see a child of the Most High King, or do you focus on your flaws? If you're like most people, you probably see the imperfections.

Women, especially, struggle with self-esteem.

Ask God to help you see yourself as He sees you. God thinks you're amazing. He doesn't mind if your thighs aren't model thin or your hair is a bit on the frizzy side. He thinks you're wonderful, and He wants you to think you're wonderful, too.

Remember that old saying, "God doesn't make any junk"? Well, it's as true today as when we learned it in vacation Bible school. You are priceless. You are far more precious than rubies. You have got it going on in God's eyes. After all, He created you!

Let God's love shine big in you, and forget about

those size 6 jeans that no longer fit. Sure, it's okay to work on your outer appearance, but don't let that consume you. Let God's love overwhelm you and spill out onto all the people around you. Get up every day, look in the mirror, and say, "I may not be perfect, but I am perfectly loved." Starting each day with that confession will put you on the road to happiness—even if you're having a bad hair day. Just grab a cute hat and greet the world with love and happiness in your heart.

Michelle Medlock Adams
Secrets of Happiness

A Vessel God Can Use

Many of the Samaritans from that town
believed in him because of the woman's
testimony, "He told me everything I ever did."

JOHN 4:39 NIV

The Samaritan woman didn't have impressive
credentials—spiritual, social, or otherwise—but
she knew enough to listen to Jesus and to consider His
claims upon her life. She didn't pretend to have all the
right answers, but she was willing to pose the right
questions. And she was willing to point people to Christ
so they, too, could make their own decisions about His
claims. She knew there was nothing within her that
would "win people to Christ," nothing she could point
to and say, "Hey, don't you want to be like me?"

What did she know? She knew she was a sinner
who had met Jesus face-to-face. That was enough to
transform her. She knew her past mistakes didn't matter. All that mattered was telling as many people as
possible about Jesus. She wasn't a perfect woman, but
she was a vessel God could use.

No matter who you are or what mistakes you've

made, the most important thing you can know about yourself is whether you have encountered Christ. Let's rejoice in the knowledge that Jesus meets us right where we live and accepts us in whatever condition we come. What we did yesterday doesn't matter; it's the future that counts. If you will only believe, God can transform you into a vessel He can use.

Donna Partow
Becoming a Vessel God Can Use

My Savior, My Bridegroom

This is how God showed his love among us: He sent his one and only Son into the world that we might live through him. This is love: not that we loved God, but that he loved us and sent his Son as an atoning sacrifice for our sins.

1 JOHN 4:9–10 NIV

Christ also hath loved us, and given Himself for us." "The Son of God. . .loved me, and gave Himself for me." Yes, Himself! What is the Bride's true and central treasure? What calls forth the deepest, brightest, sweetest thrill of love and praise? Not the Bridegroom's priceless gifts, not the robe of His resplendent righteousness, not the dowry of unsearchable riches, not the magnificence of the palace home to which He is bringing her, not the glory which she shall share with Him, but Himself! Jesus Christ, "who His own self bore our sins in His own body on the tree"; "this same Jesus," "whom having not seen, ye love"; the Son of God and the Man of Sorrows; my Savior, my Friend, my Master, my King, my Priest, my

Lord, and my God—He says, "I also for thee!" What an "I"! What power and sweetness we feel in it, so different from any human "I," for all His Godhead and all His manhood are concentrated in it, and all "for thee"!

Frances Ridley Havergal
Kept for the Master's Use

All Our Hope Is in God

For if Abraham was justified by works,
he has something to boast about, but not
before God. For what does the Scripture
say? "ABRAHAM BELIEVED GOD, AND IT WAS
CREDITED TO HIM AS RIGHTEOUSNESS."

ROMANS 4:2–3 NASB

Our work ethic is as old as the Garden of Eden. Because of sin Adam's free ride was over and he would now have to earn a living. But God said, " 'Because you have listened to the voice of your wife, and have eaten from the tree about which I commanded you, saying, "You shall not eat from it"; cursed is the ground because of you; in toil you will eat of it all the days of your life' " (Genesis 3:17 NASB).

Somehow men and women have transferred this attitude about working for things to salvation. However, salvation is not based on our "goodness," but rather on Christ's. For no matter how diligently we try to keep those Ten Commandments, we're going to fail.

God made Abraham, the one the Jews claim as their father, a promise, and he believed God. His belief wasn't merely an intellectual assent. The "Supreme God of the Universe," who made absolutely everything that Abraham now saw in his world, had deigned not only to speak to him, but He promised him an heir. The reason that Abraham could place his trust in God was because God kept His promises. No matter how impossible the situation looks, God always comes through.

Carol L. Fitzpatrick
Daily Wisdom for Women

The Comfort of God

I will pray the Father, and he shall give
you another Comforter, that he may
abide with you for ever; even the Spirit
of truth; whom the world cannot
receive, because it seeth him not, neither
knoweth him: but ye know him; for he
dwelleth with you, and shall be in you.

JOHN 14:16–17 KJV

Two little girls were talking about God, and one
said, "I know God does not love me. He could
not care for such a teeny, tiny little girl as I am."

"Dear me, sis," said the other little girl, "don't you
know that that is just what God is for—to take care of
teeny, tiny little girls who can't take care of themselves, just like us?"

"Is He?" said the first little girl. "I did not know
that. Then I don't need to worry anymore, do I?"

If any troubled doubting heart, any heart that is
fearing continually every day some form or other of
evil should read these lines, let me tell you again in
trumpet tones that this is just what the Lord Jesus

Christ is for—to care for and comfort all who mourn.

"All," remember, every single one, even you yourself, for it would not be "all" if you were left out. You may be so cast down that you can hardly lift up your head, but the apostle tells us that He is the "God that comforteth those that are cast down;" the comforting of Christ. All who mourn, all who are cast down—I love to think of such a mission of comfort in a world of mourning like ours; and I long to see every cast down and sorrowing heart comforted with this comforting of God.

Hannah Whitall Smith
The God of All Comfort

Hope in Trials, Part 1

It's best to stay in touch with both sides of an issue. A person who fears God deals responsibly with all of reality, not just a piece of it.

ECCLESIASTES 7:18 MSG

Frustrated and confused by the rumors surrounding the circumstances of our son Jason's arrest, I screamed out loud to my husband, Gene, "Don't people have anything else to do? They are getting a feeling of power out of announcing our bad news in the name of prayer requests, when they don't even have all the facts straight. This is so wrong!"

Gene is a unique personality. He never gets as animated as I do in the middle of an emotional outburst, nor does he "hit bottom" as far down as I do when things are not going well. He's steady, even, and controlled most of the time. Following my outburst that day, Gene took my hands in his two hands and said, "Carol, what's happened here is way out of our control. We are proactive people and we like to 'fix' things, but we can't change what's taken place or how people respond to it. There's not one thing we can do to stop the rumors, the stories, the opinions, and the gossiping of people. We have to let it go. This is way beyond us."

Carol Kent

When I Lay My Isaac Down

Holding Out for a Hero

Think about Jesus, who was sent to us and
is the high priest of our faith. Jesus was
faithful to God as Moses was in God's
family. . . . But Christ is faithful as a Son
over God's house. And we are God's house
if we confidently maintain our hope.

HEBREWS 3:1–2, 6 NCV

Every now and then when I can't see around the
corner of my circumstances or when I feel alone
or misunderstood, I whine for a different kind of
Messiah. One who will make all my messes disappear.
One who will answer my prayer for a husband and
children. One who will make my closest friends interested listeners, conscientious encouragers, and fatter
than me. Sometimes I just wish our Hero of a Savior
would make my life less hard.

Of course, a Savior like that only exists in fairy
tales and isn't really very heroic. A Messiah who only
serves to grant our wishes would be akin to an overly
indulgent mother who lets her child eat all the candy
he wants, stay up as late as he likes, and never makes

him accept responsibility or obey authority. Pretty soon she's got a middle-aged man with no job, no friends, and no respect for her still living in his boyhood room and demanding Twinkies for lunch. And if we had a Messiah like that, we'd be no better off.

Lisa Harper
Holding Out for a Hero

Hope in Trials, Part 2

After all this, God tested Abraham. God said, "Abraham!" "Yes?" answered Abraham. "I'm listening." He said, "Take your dear son Isaac whom you love and go to the land of Moriah. Sacrifice him there as a burnt offering on one of the mountains that I'll point out to you."

GENESIS 22:1–2 MSG

The first day I saw our son Jason in jail for the murder of his wife's ex-husband, I knew there was no way to fix things and make life as it was before. That day I took the first step in "laying my Isaac down." I admitted to God that I was helpless. I stood in the parking lot and cried until I ran out of tears. I physically opened up my hands, palm side up, and said:

"God, please help us not to waste this suffering. I could not go on living if I didn't believe I could trust You even in this. I give up my right to control the outcome of Jason's trial. I release his future to Your keeping, but God, even while I'm saying I want to relinquish my control, I want to take it back. So God,

I will let go of my control for the next minute, and if I make it that far, let's try for five more minutes, and maybe there will be a time when I will come to the end of one full day."

Carol Kent
When I Lay My Isaac Down

Content in Him

But godliness with
contentment is great gain.

I TIMOTHY 6:6 KJV

Even the strongest Christian can struggle with
discontentment. We're conditioned by the world
to want more—of everything. More money, nicer
clothes, a bigger house, a better-paying job. We're
rarely satisfied with what we have.

And when we're single, the "I Wish I Had This or
That" list can get pretty long. If we don't get the things
we long for—a spouse, children, a home, a better
car, or nicer clothes—sometimes our discontentment
shifts into overdrive. But what can we do about it?

Today, take stock of what God has already done
for you. Take a look at the areas of your life in which
you've been struggling with discontentment. Hasn't
God already given you people who pour into your
life? Hasn't He made sure you have a roof over your
head and food to eat? Has He not provided you a way
to get to and from work?

Instead of focusing on all the things you don't

have, spend some time praising Him for the things you do have. Offer the Lord any discontentment, and watch Him give you a contented heart.

Janice Hanna
Daily Encouragement for Single Women

Open Arms

"I, even I, am He who blots out your
transgressions for My own sake;
and I will not remember your sins."

ISAIAH 43:25 NKJV

I had my first car wreck when I was seventeen. I was
about an hour away from home, with a banged-up
car and a flat tire I didn't know how to change. I had
to make that dreaded phone call to my dad to let him
know what had happened. I'll never forget that moment when I saw him pull into the parking lot beside
my wrecked car. I was so scared about how he would
respond, what he would say to me. But as he walked
toward me, his arms were outstretched and he em-
braced me in a huge hug.

I often remind myself of that moment when thinking about approaching my heavenly Father when I've
done something wrong or stupid. When I call on Him,
admit what I've done, His response is like my dad's.
He longs to embrace me and fix the mess I've made.
Sure, there are consequences for my actions. But we
have a Father who is loving and who is faithful and just

to forgive us our sins when we confess them to Him. He wipes the slate clean and remembers our sin no more.

There's no reason to approach the throne of grace in fear, because it is a throne of grace. And when we find ourselves there broken over our sins, we are met with open arms.

Emily Smith
Circle of Friends

Safe in His Arms

He tends his flock like a shepherd:
He gathers the lambs in his arms
and carries them close to his heart.

ISAIAH 40:11 NIV

As a chaplain, I hear many inspiring stories from the elderly persons I serve. However, there are some days that are emotionally heavy due to their pain and struggles.

On one particularly "heavy" day, I walked into the room of a woman who was once a vibrant Christian woman. She is no longer able to feed herself, walk, or talk. As I prayed over her, I asked the Lord, "Why so much injustice, so much pain?" My eyes left her and moved to a picture hanging above her bed—a picture I had never noticed before. Jesus stood in the center surrounded by sheep. In one hand he held a staff and in the other, a lamb. The lamb was resting securely in its Shepherd's arms, cradled against His chest. At that moment, I knew the answer to my question. It's as if God was saying, "I never intended for the pain and the injustice. This world is broken, but I am here *through* the pain. I will carry her through this." It was clear—she was the lamb He held in His arms. We are the sheep that follow Him, and when one of us is in need, our Father and Shepherd picks us up and holds us close.

Today, let's be reminded that even though trials and tears may come, we are not alone. Jesus carries the helpless and dependent. He carries you and me.

Jocelyn Hamsher
Circle of Friends

Hope in Jesus

I say unto you, that likewise joy shall be
in heaven over one sinner that repenteth,
more than over ninety and nine just
persons, which need no repentance.

LUKE 15:7 KJV

Has God ever thrown a party for you? Do you
know how much doing that would thrill Him?

When a soul enters eternity by faith in Jesus,
all heaven rejoices over that new member of God's
kingdom. You might say God throws a party just for
the new believer. All heaven celebrates for each person
who comes to God through His Son. If you know Jesus, there was a day when God gave a celebration with
your name on it. Invitations went out to all heaven,
and everyone had a great time rejoicing in what God
had done in your life. It was a great day!

If you've never had such a great day in your life, it
can still happen. All you need to do is admit to God
that you need to turn your life around. Tell Him you
know you've sinned and need His forgiveness and that

you're trusting in Jesus for that forgiveness.

Do I hear a party starting?

Pamela McQuade
Daily Wisdom for the Workplace

The Power of Encouragement

"But my mouth would encourage
you; comfort from my lips
would bring you relief."

JOB 16:5 NIV

The truest earthly friends are those who share their faith in our heavenly Father. The best biblical example of friendship is that of David and Jonathan. Even though his father, King Saul, seemed determined to kill David, Jonathan told his friend, "Whatsoever thy soul desireth, I will even do it for thee" (1 Samuel 20:4 KJV). Not only did Jonathan clothe David with friendship, but he armed him as well.

In 1 Samuel, Jonathan made covenants with David as well as informed him of danger, helped to rescue him, prayed for him, appealed to God for him, and bound him to himself with promises. At their last encounter, "Jonathan. . .went to David into the wood, and strengthened his hand in God. And he said unto him, Fear not: for the hand of Saul my father shall not find thee; and thou shalt be king over Israel, and I shall be next unto thee; and that also Saul my father

knoweth. And they two made a covenant before the
Lord: and David abode in the wood, and Jonathan
went to his house" (1 Samuel 23:16–18 KJV). What a
friendship!

Each and every day, make it a point to encourage
your friends through prayer, comfort, service, listening,
and blessings. But most of all, love them, as Jonathan
loved David, as Jesus loves us.

Tap into the power of encouragement and love
from the greatest resource at our disposal, our greatest
Friend—our one and only Savior, Jesus Christ. He will
never leave us nor forsake us.

Donna K. Maltese
Power Prayers to Start Your Day

The Consecrated Life

Many are the plans in a person's heart,
but it is the LORD's purpose that prevails.

PROVERBS 19:21 NIV

Though one might hitch her "wagon to a star," so
high and noble are her aspirations, yet if after all
that star is an earthly one—knowledge, personal influence, ability, riches, honor—and her aspirations be realized and she arise high in the world, she will not find
the satisfaction in her attainments that she hoped for.
We, in our natures, are not altogether earthly; there
is in us a nature that craves to be in tune with heaven.
A life that gives exercise to this part of our being and
provides a way for the satisfying of the heart's craving
for God is the only one that brings what every person
desires—soul rest.

This consecrated life is expected of every Christian. In fact, no person can live a conscientious,
Christian life long without finding such a consecration
necessary. Either she must give herself fully to God,
or drop back into the cold, formal life that many live,
but none enjoy. Do not let anyone think that such a

devoted life is irksome, for it is not. We are so created that the heart naturally craves God, and when the powers of sin that bind have been broken and the soul has been set free to follow its right course, the highest pleasure is found in sincere service to God.

Mabel Hale
Beautiful Girlhood

Honorable Living

But God chose the foolish things
of the world to shame the wise;
God chose the weak things of the
world to shame the strong.

1 CORINTHIANS 1:27 NIV

Maybe you aren't in management, or if you are, you may feel as if you're still on a very low rung of the ladder. If you work for people who have a lot of smarts, it's easy to start feeling as if you have nothing of value to offer. After all, aren't these other folks so much better than you?

Be encouraged. God isn't just looking for the really smart, the really gifted, or the really wealthy to do His work. In fact, He seems to prefer to use the quiet, lowly, but perfectly obedient person.

You may not reach a high position in your job. Perhaps you'll stay pretty much where you are now for as long as you stay with this company. But whatever your place, if your life honors God, your faith can have a powerful impact on your workplace.

You might not get a promotion because someone

thinks you're "too honest." You might watch others pass you by because they played some office-politics games you stepped back from. But people will remember you and recognize the things you stood for. A few may even feel shame and wish they'd followed in your footsteps.

Lord, no matter where You want to use me, I want to be Your servant. Let my light shine for You today.

Pamela L. McQuade
Daily Wisdom for the Workplace

Worry No More

For the LORD will go before you.

ISAIAH 52:12 NIV

When I was a child struggling with my future, my grandmother gave me the "gift" of a worry stone. Holding this flat, oval-shaped, polished gemstone between her fingers and thumb, Grandma showed me how to rub the stone. She said that when I did this, I would gain relief from the concerns that plagued me.

As I grew, I used this worry stone when plagued by what-ifs. "What if I flunk this exam?" *Rub, rub. . .* I got a B. "What if Daddy should die?" *Rub, rub. . .* My father died on my sixteenth birthday. "What if Mark breaks up with me?" *Rub, rub. . . I* broke up with Mark.

As the years went by, I began to realize that it didn't matter how much I used the worry stone, because it changed neither the present nor the future. So I put the stone away. . .but kept the worries close at hand.

Then, years later, I visited the only church we have in Silverdale, Pennsylvania. And there, for the first time in my life, I connected with God in a personal, life-changing way. I began attending church and

Sunday school every week and diving into God's Word with an unquenchable thirst.

As I read I discovered the powerful words of Jeremiah 29:11–12: " 'For I know the plans I have for you,' declares the LORD, 'plans to prosper you and not to harm you, plans to give you hope and a future. Then you will call me and come and pray to me, and I will listen to you' " (NIV).

I was awestruck. God had plans for me! Plans to prosper and not to harm me! Plans to give me hope and a future! I began to revel in this knowledge. I realized that when worries began to come upon me, all I had to do was call upon Him, seek Him with all my heart, and tell Him all my fears of the future. He would listen and then lead me to go in the power of His divine guidance, urging me to be confident that He is before me in the going. He's got a plan for my life, full of hope in and prosperity with Him, and He will give me the power to proceed!

Donna K. Maltese
Power Prayers to Start Your Day

God in the Driver's Seat

I will instruct thee and
teach thee in the way
which thou shalt go: I will
guide thee with mine eye.

PSALM 32:8 KJV

Hannah came to a fork in the road. She had to make some life-changing decisions. The hardest part was that the decisions she made would significantly affect the lives of her loved ones. What was she to do?

God tells us that whenever we have a decision to make, He will instruct and teach us. He will not let us flounder; but as we seek His face, He will provide direction, understanding, wisdom, and insight. He will teach us the way—the road, the path, or the journey we need to take that is in our best interest. We can clearly comprehend the way we should walk because God is guiding, with His eye upon us. He is omniscient, which means He knows all things. He knows our past, our present, and our future. He sees and understands what we are not able to comprehend in our finite beings. What a blessing that an all-knowing Lord will guide us!

Tina C. Elacqua
Whispers of Wisdom for Busy Women

Hope in Resurrection

For God so loved the world that
he gave his one and only Son,
that whoever believes in him shall
not perish but have eternal life.

JOHN 3:16 NIV

W e have a man down on the play," the announcer
said during the Friday night high school football game in Rose Hill, North Carolina.

LuAnn watched helplessly as her son collapsed on
the field and didn't get up. After a few moments she
rushed from the stands and held Will in her arms as
he took his last breath. A concussion of the heart, the
doctors explained later.

*O God, how can a mother bear the loss of her precious
son?* I prayed.

Then He reminded me of Mary, who watched her
son, battered and bleeding, nailed to a cruel Roman
cross.

"Yes, Lord," I said. "But Jesus came back to life.
Will won't."

I kept my questioning to myself, knowing it
wouldn't help anyone.

A few days later, LuAnn courageously spoke at her son's funeral. She stood before a crowded congregation and told about Jesus, whom Will loved.

"Accept Jesus as your Savior and receive eternal life," she urged.

Thirty people came to faith that day.

The following week LuAnn spoke at the opponent's school assembly. Again she shared the Gospel, and many boys and girls came to Christ.

It was an extraordinary moment when I realized that while Will was not physically raised from the dead, resurrection power took place as hundreds of souls experienced new life in Christ through his story.

Sharon Jaynes
Extraordinary Moments with God

Created by God

So God created mankind in his own
image, in the image of God he created
them; male and female he created them.

GENESIS 1:27 NIV

A whole new year stretches out before you, like a crisp carpet of newly fallen snow. What kind of footprints will you leave? Maybe your strides will be gigantic leaps of faith. Or perhaps you will take tiny steps of slow, steady progress. Some imprints might even be creative expressions, woman-sized angels in the snow.

You are a woman; you were created in God's own image. But that isn't the message our world peddles. So what does it mean to be created in God's image? For starters, you have imagination, intellect, and most importantly, a soul. That's the deepest part of your being, where you long to feel whole, loved, cherished, and understood.

But hold the phone: God made you so that He might have an ongoing relationship with you. You need Him and He's promised to always be there for you. Isn't that the kind of life companion you've searched for?

On her fifty-fifth birthday a close friend confided in me that she's never felt really loved by anyone. "That's not true," I told her. "God loves you." Hopefully during this year she'll understand that God has been there all along. She just didn't take time to look in His Word. She didn't take time to feel His love.

Carol L. Fitzpatrick
Daily Wisdom for Women

Let Go

So do not fear, for I am with you;
do not be dismayed, for I am your God.
I will strengthen you and help you; I will
uphold you with my righteous right hand.

ISAIAH 41:10 NIV

D o you recollect the delicious sense of rest with
which you have sometimes gone to bed at night,
after a day of great exertion and weariness? How
delightful was the sensation of relaxing every muscle
and letting your body go in a perfect abandonment of
ease and comfort! The strain of the day had ceased, for
a few hours at least, and the work of the day had been
laid off. You no longer had to hold up an aching head
or a weary back. You trusted yourself to the bed in an
absolute confidence, and it held you up, without effort
or strain or even thought, on your part. You rested!

But suppose you had doubted the strength or the
stability of your bed and had dreaded each moment to
find it giving way beneath you and landing you on the
floor; would you have rested then? Would not every
muscle have been strained in a fruitless effort to hold

yourself up, and would not the weariness have been greater than if you had not gone to bed at all?

Let this analogy teach you what it means to rest in the Lord. Let your souls lie down upon the couch of His sweet will, as your bodies lie down in their beds at night. Relax every strain, and lay off every burden. Let yourself go in a perfect abandonment of ease and comfort, sure that, since He holds you up, you are perfectly safe. Your part is simply to rest. His part is to sustain you; and He cannot fail.

Hannah Whitall Smith
The Christian's Secret of a Happy Life

Financial Strain

"No one can serve two masters.
Either you will hate the one and love
the other, or you will be devoted to
the one and despise the other. You
cannot serve both God and money."

MATTHEW 6:24 NIV

Do you ever get nervous when you watch the news and see reports about the stock market? Does your head spin when you see the prices rise at the gas pump? Can you feel your heart race when you look at your bills in comparison to your bank statement? Even though many of our day-to-day activities depend on money, it's important to remember that money is not a provider or sustainer. Only God can provide for you and sustain you. When we begin to focus on and worry about money, then we are telling God that we don't trust Him.

As you feel yourself start to worry about money, stop and change your focus from wealth to God. Thank Him for what He has provided for you and then humbly ask Him to give you wisdom about your financial situation. Be at peace as you remember that you can absolutely trust God to provide for you and to sustain you.

Sarah Mae Ratliff
Daily Encouragement for Single Women

Step into Your Dreams

This resurrection life you received from God is not a timid, grave-tending life. It's adventurously expectant, greeting God with a childlike "What's next, Papa?"

ROMANS 8:15 MSG

In the early 1950s, Lillian Vernon spent five hundred dollars on her first advertisement, offering monogrammed belts and handbags. That one ad produced a $32,000 profit! Today—more than fifty years later—Lillian Vernon is still selling gift items through a very successful catalog sales program. In fact, her company now generates more than $250 million in sales every year.

But what if Lillian Vernon hadn't run that small ad? What if she hadn't taken that risk? Well, she wouldn't be a millionaire, and lots of folks would have to find another catalog to use for their annual Christmas shopping.

Maybe God has put a dream in your heart that is so big you haven't even shared it with anyone. So what's stopping you? Why aren't you running that ad like Lillian Vernon?

If you're like most women, fear is holding you back. Fear is a very real emotion. It can get a grip on you that won't let go—until you make it let go through the Word of God. Say out loud, "I can do all things through Christ who strengthens me. I am the head and not the tail. I am more than a conqueror."

Remind yourself of who you are in Christ Jesus on a daily basis. God has crowned you with His favor. So grab hold of God's promises, put fear behind you, and step into your dreams. Pretty soon, you'll be sharing your success story!

Michelle Medlock Adams
Secrets of Beauty

Singing the Blue Jeans Blues

Not that I have already obtained all this,
or have already arrived at my goal, but I
press on to take hold of that for which
Christ Jesus took hold of me.

PHILIPPIANS 3:12 NIV

We've all been there. You go to the mall with high hopes and high self-esteem, ready to buy a new pair of jeans. Seventy-two pairs later, your legs are raw from trying them on and your self-esteem is lower than a snake's belly.

Jeans are a part of every gal's wardrobe, but finding a pair that fits every curve and hides every bulge can be challenging.

Still, we press on—determined to find the jeans that won't make our hind ends look flat and wide. Sometimes this quest may take days, even weeks. But, eventually, we will succeed. We're women—shopping challenges don't faze us.

If only we were that steadfast when it comes to other areas of our lives—especially spiritual battles. Have you found yourself throwing in the faith towel before you see your victory come to pass?

It's easy to do. Evangelist Chip Brim once shared that God had shown him a vision of Christians on a football field. They were collapsing on the one-yard line. They were so close to their breakthroughs, but they simply grew weary and quit inches from their victory.

Chip said it made him very sad to see so many Christians quitting before they'd realized their breakthroughs. The Bible says you can do all things through Christ Jesus. Don't quit just short of your victory. The reward is even better than finding that perfect pair of blue jeans.

Michelle Medlock Adams
Secrets of Beauty

Your Song Is Coming

"My food," said Jesus, "is to do the will of him who sent me and to finish his work."

JOHN 4:34 NIV

After being a Christian more than thirty years, the truth was I wasn't able to handle everything on my plate, but I was making myself sick trying. I thought God would take me through, but this time was different. I just wanted to cry and run away from life. I'd thought I was a maturing Christian, but now I wasn't so sure. How could I be and feel this way?

Did you know it's entirely possible to be desperately thirsty in body, mind, and spirit and not know it? I've hardly met a woman who hasn't been there at least once.

Jesus experienced deep thirst, too. He was thirsty to do the will of God, something otherworldly. Thirsty to bring His Father praise and honor and worship, to bring songs of joy to the throne of God. Not even His disciples knew what that meant until later.

We aren't born with that kind of thirst. We're reborn with it. The greatest joy in our journey toward renewal is recovering our thirst for God's glory, our own song of praise to Him.

You may not feel ready to sing anything today. No one does when she is flat-out. Add a dose of depression to the mix, and you have one songless canary. For now, know that your song is coming. It is unique to you, a special gift from God.

Virelle Kidder

Meet Me at the Well

Vocalizing a Prayer

And when you are praying, do not use
meaningless repetition as the Gentiles
do, for they suppose that they will be
heard for their many words.

MATTHEW 6:7 NASB

Remember kneeling beside your bed and praying when you were a kid? Why did it all seem so simple then? We just talked to God like He was really there and kept our requests short and simple.

Then, as you got older, the lengthy and spiritual prayers of the "older saints" became intimidating. So where's the balance? Reading a little further in this passage from Matthew, at verse 9, Jesus gives us His own example for prayer. If you can remember the acrostic ACTS, you'll have an excellent formula for prayer: Adoration, Confession, Thanksgiving, and Supplication.

As we come before the Lord, we first need to honor Him as Creator, Master, Savior, and Lord. Reflect on who He is and praise Him. And because we're human, we need to confess and repent of our daily sins. Following this we should be in a mode of thanksgiving.

Finally, our prayer requests should be upheld. My usual order for requests is self, family members, and life's pressing issues. Keeping a prayer journal allows for a written record of God's answers.

Your prayers certainly don't have to be elaborate or polished. God does not judge your way with words. He knows your heart. He wants to hear from you.

Carol L. Fitzpatrick
Daily Wisdom for Women

Always Sunshine

So we fix our eyes not on what is seen,
but on what is unseen, since what is seen
is temporary, but what is unseen is eternal.

———————————

2 CORINTHIANS 4:18 NIV

There is never a moment when I am absent from
the scene of your life. Your feeling of separation
does not make it so. It is like the sunshine. Clouds
enshroud the earth and you say the sun is not shining.
This is not true. The sun is *always* shining. The truth is
that because it is a cloudy day, you cannot *see* the sun
shining. Even so, My grace is always pouring down
upon you, and in moments when your own spirit may
not discern it, My love is nonetheless constant and real.

Rejoice in Me, for truly I am all you need. I am
light and life, hope and peace. I am the joy-giver. My
presence is with you, and wherever I am, there is
harmony. I am your deliverer and the source of all
your strength. You can never ask beyond My power to
provide.

Your joy may be restored at any moment as you
brush aside the clouds of earth by recapturing the

strength of the times when you have felt the warmth
of the sunshine, yes, even been blinded by the power
of its rays.

Frances J. Roberts
On the Highroad of Surrender

Focusing on Pleasing God

Am I now trying to win the approval
of human beings, or of God? Or am I
trying to please people? If I were still
trying to please people, I would not
be a servant of Christ.

GALATIANS 1:10 NIV

We all have those days when it seems we are
disappointing everyone around us. Your co-
worker expected you to drop your projects and help
her with hers, but you had hoped she would be able
to do the same for you. Your best friend let you bor-
row her favorite handmade scarf for a date, and you
accidentally spilled your café mocha on it. Your sister
called to ask if you'd watch your niece while she takes
your nephew to a doctor's appointment, but you've
already made plans for the afternoon. There are even
days when we feel that we have been doing almost
more than we can do and still we have people dis-
pleased and angry with us.

Praise God that He sees us as valuable, even
though we don't always do things perfectly. Thank

God that He doesn't expect us to say yes to every request that we receive. Focus your time on listening to how God wants you to serve Him and the people in your life, but don't be discouraged when you discover you can't please everyone.

Sarah Mae Ratliff

Daily Encouragement for Single Women

Choosing Hope

Though you have made me see troubles,
many and bitter, you will restore my
life again; from the depths of the earth
you will again bring me up.

PSALM 71:20 NIV

When I was six weeks of age a slight cold caused an inflammation of the eyes, which appeared to demand the attention of the family physician; but he not being at home, a stranger was called. He recommended the use of hot poultices, which ultimately destroyed the sense of sight. When this sad misfortune became known throughout our neighborhood, the unfortunate man thought it best to leave; and we never heard of him again. But I have not for a moment, in more than eighty-five years, felt a spark of resentment against him because I have always believed from my youth to this very moment that the good Lord, in His infinite mercy, by this means consecrated me to the work that I am still permitted to do. When I remember His mercy and loving-kindness; when I have been blessed above the common lot of mortals; and when happiness has touched the deep places of my soul, how can I repine? "The light of the body is the eye: if therefore thine eye be single, thy whole body shall be full of light. But if thine eye be evil, thy whole body shall be full of darkness. If therefore the light that is in thee be darkness, how great is that darkness!"

Fanny Crosby
Memories of Eighty Years

Caring for the Temple

Honor God with your body.

1 CORINTHIANS 6:20 NLT

Our bodies are an amazing gift from God. Without any thought or effort on our parts, our hearts beat life-giving blood throughout our veins, providing us with the energy to accomplish the thousands of tasks we do each day. Our brains give the commands; our bodies obey. But these incredible structures aren't maintenance free. Just as we are to be good stewards of our resources of time and money, we should also be good stewards of our bodies. God's Word calls them a temple.

When we are busy meeting the needs of others, we often neglect to care for ourselves. But God wants us to treat our bodies with care and respect. This means exercising regularly, eating good food, and getting enough rest. These are simple things, but the dividends are high, for when we treat our bodies right, they treat us right in return.

Joanna Bloss
To Love and to Cherish

The Sweetness of Little Flowers

They have freely scattered their gifts to the
poor, their righteousness endures forever;
their horn will be lifted high in honor.

PSALM 112:9 NIV

For a long time I wondered why God showed partiality, why all souls don't receive the same amount of graces. I was astounded to see Him lavish extraordinary favors on the saints who had offended Him such as Saint Paul and Saint Augustine, and whom He so to speak forced to receive His graces. Or when I read the life of saints whom our Lord was pleased to embrace from the cradle to the grave; without leaving in their path any obstacles that might hinder them from rising toward Him, and granting these souls such favors that they were unable to tarnish the immaculate brightness of their baptismal robes, I wondered: why poor primitive people, for example, were dying in great numbers without even having heard the name of God pronounced.

Jesus consented to teach me this mystery. He placed before my eyes the book of nature; I understood that all the flowers that He created are beautiful. The brilliance of the rose and the whiteness of the lily don't take away the perfume of the lowly violet or the delightful simplicity of the daisy. . . . I understood that if all the little flowers wanted to be roses, nature would lose its springtime adornment, and the fields would no longer be sprinkled with little flowers.

So it is in the world of souls, which is Jesus' garden. He wanted to create great saints who could be compared to lilies and roses. But He also created little ones, and these ought to be content to be daisies or violets destined to gladden God's eyes when He glances down at His feet. Perfection consists in doing His will, in being what He wants us to be.

Saint Therese of Lisieux
The Story of a Soul

Repent and Be Restored

And I will restore to you the years that
the locust hath eaten, the cankerworm,
and the caterpillar, and the palmerworm,
my great army which I sent among you.

JOEL 2:25 KJV

Throughout scripture we encounter a divine para-
dox, an apparent contradiction in the way God
intervenes in human history: the God who chastens
His people is the same God who turns around and
blesses them.

We see this over and over in the history of Israel.
God directs Israel; Israel follows for a while but then
turns away and commits sin. God chastises His people,
destroying their crops or sending them into exile.
When they repent, He has pity on them and blesses
them again.

The key is repentance.

Our hearts must turn from ourselves to our Lord.
God is so gracious, forgiving, and loving that a mus-
tard seed of repentance grows a whole tree of blessing.
God restores what was lost, even when He knows

there will be future failures.

Have the locusts been eating away at your marriage? Have there been mistakes and failures? Has your pride caused contentions in your house? If so, repent. Turn from your foolish ways and obey Him.

He will cause His face to shine upon you. And will restore the years the locusts ate.

Helen Widger Middlebrooke

To Love and to Cherish

Jesus, Our Lifeline

The name of the LORD is a
strong fortress; the godly
run to him and are safe.

———◆———

PROVERBS 18:10 NLT

The greatest moment of your life can be when
everything seems finished for you. That is the
moment when you lay your weak hand in the strong
hand of Jesus. For Jesus can make life and death—
present and future—victorious! He can give you
eternal life; not only life in heaven, but life right now.

It is as when you have fallen in the sea and you
think, *Now I will surely drown. I can swim perhaps an hour,
but then I will sink!* A lifeline is the only thing that can
help you then.

I found that when you are drowning in the terrific
misery of the world, Jesus is everything for you—your
only lifeline. When you think you have lost everything,
then you can be found by Jesus Christ.

He died for you, He lives for you, and He loves
you more than any human being can love. I have told
people about Him for thirty-three years, in sixty-four

countries, and in all that time nobody has ever told me he was sorry he asked Jesus to come into his life. You won't be sorry either.

Corrie ten Boom
Oh, How He Loves You

Words of Wisdom
from Eleanor Roosevelt

As God's chosen people, holy and dearly loved, clothe yourselves with compassion, kindness, humility, gentleness and patience.

COLOSSIANS 3:12 NIV

Eleanor Roosevelt has been called the most revered woman of her generation. She not only gave birth to six children, but also served as a dynamic political helpmate to her husband, Franklin Delano Roosevelt.

Eleanor Roosevelt literally transformed the role of First Lady, holding press conferences, traveling to all parts of the country, giving lectures and radio broadcasts, and expressing her opinions in a daily syndicated newspaper column called "My Day." You might say that she was a woman on a mission, a servant to humankind, and a role model for all women.

Knowing of her accomplishments, it was very interesting to discover Mrs. Roosevelt was a very shy and awkward child. It wasn't until she began attending a distinguished school in England that she began to develop self-confidence. During that self-discovery phase, she wrote, "No matter how plain a woman may be, if truth and loyalty are stamped upon her face, all will be attracted to her."

What wise words from such a young teen, huh? If only we all understood that truth.

If you're feeling plain, unworthy, unattractive, and unnoticed—give yourself a makeover from the inside out. Ask God to develop the fruits of the Spirit within you, and allow the Lord to fill you with His love. Pretty soon, you'll be confident and irresistible. And you'll make a difference every place you go!

Michelle Medlock Adams
Secrets of Beauty

Not Enough to Go Around

Cast thy burden upon the LORD,
and he shall sustain thee: he shall
never suffer the righteous to be moved.

PSALM 55:22 KJV

Did you ever walk on a balance beam when you were a child? I loved gymnastics when I was growing up, but I was never very good on the balance beam. I'd topple off to one side quite often. You know what's ironic? I'm still having trouble with that whole balancing concept. Only now I'm having trouble balancing my personal and professional life. How about you? Maybe you're an employee, a wife, a mom, a friend, a daughter, a sister, an aunt, a church volunteer, etc. And you're not sure how to be all of those things at one time. If you are all those things, welcome to the Sisterhood—the "Sisterhood of There's Not Enough of Me to Go Around."

There are days when I wonder how I am supposed to accomplish everything that is on my plate. But you know what? I'm not! God never intended me to do this by myself. And He never intended for you to go it alone, either. The Word tells us that we can do all things through Christ who gives us strength. All means all, right?

So no matter how many roles you're fulfilling today, don't sweat it! God will help you.

Michelle Medlock Adams
Daily Wisdom for Working Women

Put On the New

And provide for those who grieve in
Zion—to bestow on them a crown of
beauty instead of ashes, the oil of joy
instead of mourning, and a garment of
praise instead of a spirit of despair.
They will be called oaks of righteousness,
a planting of the LORD for the
displayof his splendor.

ISAIAH 61:3 NIV

I have to admit I'm a sucker for those fashion makeover shows. I love the one where the guy and girl
ambush some poor unsuspecting person and help
them buy a brand-new wardrobe. But the catch is that
the victims have to be willing to throw away all of
their old clothes.

I'm amazed that anyone would put up a fight—but
they almost always do! I mean, what on earth could be
hanging in someone's closet that they wouldn't gladly
toss out to replace it with something new? And yet
I have seen people pleading to keep their worn-out
bunny slippers and tie-dyed T-shirts.

When you think about it, aren't we just as crazy? Our Father God has—through Christ—given us the opportunity to shed a spirit of heaviness and replace it with a garment of praise. But we sometimes have trouble letting go of the heaviness.

And that's when He comes to the rescue again, taking us by the hand, guiding us, and gently helping us cast off the old and put on the new.

Suzie Thomas
Circle of Friends

Claiming God's Promise

And the LORD spake unto Moses, saying,
The daughters of Zelophehad speak right:
thou shalt surely give them a possession
of an inheritance among their father's
brethren; and thou shalt cause the inheritance of their father to pass unto them.

NUMBERS 27:6–7 KJV

What confidence the five daughters of Zelophehad had in God's provisions for women!
Imagine the courage required for them to ask their
leaders to deviate from established legal tradition as
they petitioned: "Why should the name of our father
be removed from among his family because he had no
son? Give us a possession among our father's brothers"
(Numbers 27:4 NKJV).

The laws God gave to the Hebrews were essential
in maintaining law and order in the community and
the property rights for individuals. This was crucial in
ensuring that a family endured and prospered. Nor-
mally, such property passed through the sons.

Zelophehad was a descendant of Joseph, making his

lineage vital to the community. While he died without sons, he did leave behind five daughters. According to existing law, Zelophehad's possessions were to pass to his brothers. Instead, these five women stepped out and appealed to Moses so that their father's lineage could continue.

When Moses then turned to God for an answer, the Lord agreed with Zelophehad's daughters: "If a man dies and has no son, then you shall cause his inheritance to pass to his daughter" (Numbers 27:8 NKJV). Only if a man had no children would his brothers inherit. In a patriarchal society in which women had few rights, this was a radical change. This God-dictated shift in Hebrew law reveals how much He cares for women.

Ramona Richards
Secrets of Confidence

What's Holding You Back?

Thank you for making me so wonderfully complex! Your workmanship is marvelous—how well I know it.

PSALM 139:14 NLT

Fanny Crosby, the author of more than nine thousand hymns and another one thousand secular poems and songs, never let her physical challenges stop the call she felt on her life. And she never let her disability become a hindrance in her relationship with God.

Born in 1820, Fanny had her vision at birth. But at six weeks, she suffered an eye inflammation. The family's usual doctor wasn't available, so they sought help from a man who claimed to be medically qualified to help. He put a poultice on Fanny's eyes, leaving the infant's eyes scarred. The "doctor" left town—and Fanny blind.

Growing up blind wasn't easy, but Fanny didn't blame God for her situation. She didn't ask, "Why me?" Instead, she determined in her heart to make a difference in this world.

When adversity happens in life, people respond in

different ways. Some get angry with God. And some become even more determined to reach their goals and dreams—like Fanny.

If you've been dealing with a painful disability or if you've been emotionally crippled due to circumstances beyond your control, God cares. Despite your troubles, God's plan for you has never changed, and His plan is a good one!

If you don't know the plan that God has for you, ask Him to show you. Tell Him that you are ready to carry out all that He has for you to do. Like Fanny, you are an important part of His overall plan in this world.

Michelle Medlock Adams
Secrets of Beauty

Renewed Hope

Answer me, GOD; O answer me
and reveal to this people that
you are GOD, the true God.

I KINGS 18:37 MSG

Immediately after God opened a major door of ministry for Elijah, he got new instructions. "God then told Elijah, 'Get out of here, and fast. Head east and hide out at the Kerith Ravine. . . . You can drink fresh water from the brook; I've ordered the ravens to feed you.' Elijah obeyed God's orders." But after a while, "the brook dried up" (summary of 1 Kings 17:2–7 MSG).

Did you get that? After what appeared to be a big-time opportunity for powerful and visible ministry, God sent Elijah to the brook—but it dried up. It shut down. It quit meeting his needs. It left him thirsty.

When the brook dries up, dreams shatter. Hopes are dashed. God seems far away. We feel abandoned by people we were hoping would satisfy our needs. But more than that, we feel rejected by a God who should have intervened in our situation. The One who is Living Water and says He loves us and wants to meet our needs has allowed the brook to dry up.

But the end of the story reminds us that it is never too late to resolve our fear in a God-honoring way. As we experience the deep sorrow of rejection and abandonment, our brokenness before God leads to a surrender of our stubborn, self-reliant will and paves the road for future faith-filled decisions that bring healing, acceptance, and nonpossessive love.

Carol Kent
Tame Your Fears

Receiving God's Embrace

See what great love the Father has
lavished on us, that we should be called
children of God! And that is what we are!

1 JOHN 3:1 NIV

Some people are born "huggers." They greet family members and complete strangers in the same way—with a hug. They just can't help themselves. They must lavish love on those around them. They must demonstrate affection. Most of us would agree that the closer the relationship, the more meaningful the hug. Can you imagine receiving an embrace from our heavenly Father, the God of the universe?

God lavished His love on us when He sent Jesus to earth. Jesus' sacrificial death on our behalf paved the way for adoption into God's family by faith. When we receive the gift of Jesus, we become children of God. We are no longer strangers. We are no longer alienated from a holy God. We have become family!

As you ponder God's great love for you, picture Jesus hanging on the cross. With arms outstretched, He not only came to embrace the world with God's love; He came to embrace you! Will you receive God's hug? The unconditional love of our Creator is the greatest gift we could ever receive. Will you allow His love to be lavished upon you? Receive the embrace of your heavenly Father today!

Julie Rayburn
To Love and to Cherish

He's Always There

Where can I go from your Spirit?
Where can I flee from your presence?
If I go up to the heavens, you are there;
if I make my bed in the depths,
you are there.

PSALM 139:7–8 NIV

I won't leave you," I gently promised my young son for about the fifth time. A haphazard glance around the playground had just terrified him into thinking I had gone without him and he desperately needed my reassurance. "I am right here," I told him again and again when he continued to cling to me. I stifled an impatient sigh. How many times did I need to tell him the same thing? Why didn't he believe me? Suddenly, the irony hit me. What I was saying to my son sounded incredibly familiar. How many times does my God tell me He won't leave me? And how many times do I stubbornly ignore His reassurances?

In His Word, God tells me over and over that He will not leave me. " 'I will never leave you nor forsake you,' " He lovingly reminds me in Joshua 1:5. "For the

LORD loves the just and will not forsake his faithful ones," He says again in Psalm 37:28. And when I cry out to Him again to make sure He's still there, He patiently directs me to Psalm 37:25: "I have never seen the righteous forsaken or their children begging bread." I have to reluctantly admit that I am more like a six-year-old than I would like to be. I, too, need to be continually reminded that God is right here beside me.

Janine Miller
Circle of Friends

Confidence to Go Beyond

"Have I not commanded you? Be strong
and of good courage; do not be afraid,
nor be dismayed, for the LORD your God
is with you wherever you go."

JOSHUA 1:9 NKJV

Sometimes confidence is found in the most unlikely
of places. For writer, speaker, and interior designer
Ann Platz, this place was the pantry of her new home.

The author of thirteen books, Ann speaks regularly
to a variety of groups and has even written about the
courage of women who have shown great faith in the
face of adversity.

Past successes, however, don't always mean having
confidence in future endeavors. Women who seek to
grow and expand, in both their faith and their personal goals, often find themselves facing tasks that far
exceed their current abilities. Or so they may believe.

Ann found an answer to those doubts when she
moved into her new home. Ann writes, "I discovered
this scripture, Joshua 1:9, printed on a business-sized
card, in the pantry of my new home. The house had

belonged to the estate of a woman I greatly admired, Mrs. Grace Kinser. Later I realized that this message 'left behind' would be a life message to me. I framed the card. Many a day I have been challenged beyond my abilities and have sought great spiritual strength and confidence from this printed message of grace from Grace."

When we believe our own abilities will fail us, we can turn our minds and hearts outward, relying on the One who never fails. God, who is always with us, will give us the strength and courage to face—and conquer—whatever challenges lie before us.

Ramona Richards
Secrets of Confidence

Let's Make a Deal

"But if serving the LORD seems undesir-
able to you, then choose for yourselves
this day whom you will serve."

JOSHUA 24:15 NIV

Let's Make a Deal! Remember the game show? One popular game of suspense that occurred frequently on the show was when a contestant was asked to choose one of three doors without knowing what was concealed behind it. After vacillating back and forth, the decision was made and the contestant anxiously waited to see what was behind the door. Sometimes it would be a new car received with great enthusiasm. At other times, the outcome was a hoax met with a disappointing sigh.

What if you were told you could choose one of three doors but unlike the contestant on the game show, you were told what's behind each one. Would you do it? Read on.

Behind door one—your past. You can continue to let past abuse, broken relationships, or previous failures keep you held back and tied down. Or, you can break free of the past and choose something different like:

Door two—the present. You can choose to focus on the present and get caught up in all this world has to offer. You can pursue wealth, popularity, fun, and excitement. This present world has a lot to offer. "Is there something else to consider?" you ask. Yes. It's behind door three!

Door three—God and His plan for you. "Really? Does God really have something unique in mind for me?" The answer is yes. He has a dream for you to pursue. The choice is up to you.

Bobbie Rill
Circle of Friends

The Power of Creative Vision

Be careful how you live. Don't live like
fools, but like those who are wise.
Make the most of every opportunity.

EPHESIANS 5:15–16 NLT

Many people look back upon their lives as a
series of missed opportunities. Are you one of
them?

Take the following steps to ensure that you make
the most of every opportunity in the future:

First, pray for creative vision. Take your ideas to
Jesus, the One by whom "all things were created. . .
visible and invisible" (Colossians 1:16 NKJV). Jesus
is just waiting for you to prayerfully present your
dreams and ideas to Him.

Second, listen expectantly. After you have prayed
for creative vision, be still, open your mind, and expect
God to speak to you. God shares your dreams with you.

Third, begin to pay attention to what is around
you. Keep your eyes open to the "creative possibilities"
surrounding you!

Fourth, be resourceful. Sometimes, when God is

calling us into a certain area, we need to make our own opportunities.

And last, have courage. Sometimes it seems easier to stay anchored in the place where we feel the most comfortable. But that place may not be where God wants us to be. Courage is needed to set sail into unknown waters.

Pray for creative vision, expect God to speak to you, pay attention to the winds blowing around you, be resourceful, and then courageously set sail, confident that God has given you the ability to take advantage of every opportunity He affords you. Remember that you are never alone: God will be with you throughout your voyage, steering you through every ocean!

Donna K. Maltese
Power Prayers to Start Your Day

Waiting in Hope

Wait on the LORD; be of good courage,
and He shall strengthen your heart;
wait, I say, on the LORD!

PSALM 27:14 NKJV

It's taken me decades to realize that waiting is more a posture of the heart than tapping my foot over the passage of time. It's willingness to yield to the One who loves me most, bowing to His Lordship—a requirement for learning anything deeper about God. Always open to our cry, the King of heaven is never in a hurry and expects to be trusted. His answers are always best, perfectly on time, and are worlds better than anything I could have imagined on my own.

We have friends who wait today while cancer's tentacles claim a spouse, or a tumor expands inside a son-in-law's head, or a beloved child changes course in sexual orientation or waits in a prison cell. What are they to do? How does any child of God wait quietly while the guillotine seems poised above?

Perhaps by grace. Perhaps by exhausting every repentant thought, every prayer for change. Then what remains is to lay our head on His lap and rest in His care. "Though he slay me, yet will I hope in him," said Job at a similar moment (13:15 NIV). Only by grace is quietness and confidence our strength—and only when His strange and holy presence takes over completely. Such submission is not learned in seasons of blessing, but when every alternative is gone, we find He is enough, and His way is best.

Virelle Kidder
The Best Life Ain't Easy, But It's Worth It

Giving Our Best

Honor the Lord with your wealth,
with the firstfruits of all your crops;
then your barns will be filled to
overflowing, and your vats will brim
over with new wine.

PROVERBS 3:9–10 NIV

When God talks about pure offerings, He's dead serious. And when He says to give Him the firstfruits of our produce, He's referring to the very best, not inexpensive substitutes.

Of course, not as many people make a living in agriculture anymore. We don't all pay our bills by farming or put jars of olives in the collection plate on Sunday. And the closest most of us come to sheep is wearing wool in the winter. So I've written "heart and mind" next to Proverbs 3:9–10 in my Bible. Because I think the context of *firstfruits* can be expanded to include our time and attention.

In other words, we should be thinking about God more than anyone else. He should be more important to us than anything. Instead of slinking toward Him with scratch-and-dent sacrifices, we should run to Him with offerings we've spent our whole allowance on. And we should be able to stand before Him with big silly grins—like kindergarteners with a plaster-of-paris handprint we made all by ourselves—knowing that He's going to love what we've brought Him!

Lisa Harper
Tough Love, Tender Mercies

Hope in Endurance

No discipline seems pleasant at the time,
but painful. Later on, however, it produces
a harvest of righteousness and peace for
those who have been trained by it.

HEBREWS 12:11 NIV

My child, do not flinch under My disciplines.
I never send more than you can endure, but
often I know that is more than you think. Can you
accept the cup of suffering as readily as you embrace
joy? You can do so in greater degrees as your trust in
Me increases. If you know I only send what is for your
good, you will see all things good and will know it
passes through My love as it comes to you.

Through much tribulation I am bringing My
chosen to perfection. Be not amazed when challenges
present themselves. I am building your fortitude, and
the day will come when you will be grateful for every
lesson learned in the school of affliction.

My love never fails, even when it brings you pain.
My love endures all things (1 Corinthians 13:7), and
it will teach you to do likewise. It is in the patient

endurance of affliction that the soul is seasoned with grace. It is a barren life that holds only happiness. Saints are not nurtured by levity. Hope does not spring from good fortune.

Hold sacred *every experience*.

Frances J. Roberts
On the Highroad of Surrender

You Are Wanted

So God created mankind in his own image,
in the image of God he created them;
male and female he created them.

GENESIS 1:27 NIV

Are you a creative person? Do you like to arrange photos in artful ways to make a scrapbook? Maybe you enjoy fashioning beads and metals into a beautiful piece of jewelry. Perhaps arranging flowers in a vase gives you a sense of joy and satisfaction.

Think for a moment about what started your endeavor. At the very basic level, you wanted whatever it was that you set out to create. One woman paints because she wants a picture. Another knits because she wants a scarf.

Have you ever thought about why God created us? Genesis records how God formed the earth, sea, and sky. He filled them with fish and birds, plants and animals. And when everything was ready for human habitation, He created man and woman.

God wanted us. That has been His desire from the beginning. When sin separated us from God, He made a way back by sending His Son to die for us. The precious blood of Christ holds the power of redemption and reconciliation.

Jesus prayed in John 17:24 (NIV), "Father, I want those you have given me to be with me where I am, and to see my glory." Jesus wants to be with us! If we have given our hearts to Him, we belong to Him.

If you're here, then you were made.
If you were made, then you are loved.
If you are loved. . .
There's a reason that you're here.

You are wanted!

Julie Hufstetler
Singer, Songwriter

Unwavering Hope

But Jesus immediately said to them:
"Take courage! It is I. Don't be afraid."
"Lord, if it's you," Peter replied,
"tell me to come to you on the water."
"Come," he said. Then Peter got down
out of the boat, walked on the water
and came toward Jesus. But when he
saw the wind, he was afraid and, beginning to sink, cried out, "Lord, save me!"
Immediately Jesus reached out his hand
and caught him. "You of little faith,"
he said, "why did you doubt?"

MATTHEW 14:27–31 NIV

Before this event occurred, Peter had already seen Jesus heal a leper, mute demoniacs, his own mother-in-law, and more. He'd even been present when Jesus demonstrated His power over nature by calming the wind. Still, after witnessing all these miracles, Peter wavered on the water. Why? E. M. Bounds provides this answer: "Doubt and fear are the twin foes of faith."

Knowing this disciple would eventually sink, why did

Jesus invite him out of the boat? Matthew Henry writes, "Christ bid [Peter to] come, not only that he might walk upon the water, and so know Christ's power, but that he might sink, and so know his own weakness."

Knowing that even Peter doubted at times provides us with a little relief. Again, Matthew Henry writes: "The strongest faith and the greatest courage have a mixture of fear. Those that can say, *Lord, I believe;* must say, *Lord, help my unbelief*."

Like Peter, when we begin to panic and find ourselves sinking, we must cry out in specific and fervent prayer to Jesus, saying, "Lord, save me!" And as Jesus did with Peter, He will *immediately* reach out and save us.

By keeping our eyes off our difficulties and fixed on Jesus, we will overcome our doubts and fears and find ourselves walking on the living water of His power, His Word, and His promises. We must be unwavering in our faith that God will uphold us no matter what our trial.

Donna K. Maltese
Power Prayers to Start Your Day

Let Your Joy Shine!

But let all those that put their trust in thee rejoice: let them ever shout for joy, because thou defendest them: let them also that love thy name be joyful in thee.

PSALM 5:11 KJV

If there is anything that is missing from the Christian home these days, it's a smile.

Weighed down by unreasonable expectations, impossible schedules, and just the daily grind of life, we become stressed and sullen. Smiles disappear at the first hint of tension.

Why do we open our homes to the thieving pressures that rob us of joy? Why do we so easily forget the great things that God has done and is doing for us?

God is our redeemer. Our defender. Our rock. Our high tower. Our hope. Our deliverer. Our shield. Our strength. Our salvation.

We are forgiven. Justified. Sanctified. Made holy.

Our bodies are the temple of the Holy Spirit. He is in us, and we are in Him. Nothing—death, life, angels, principalities, powers, the future, the past, things in the heavens or the deep, or any other creature (even our faithless selves)—absolutely nothing can separate us from the love of God in Christ Jesus our Lord.

If we would truly grasp just one of these truths, our lives and our faces would be light and cheerful.

Our burdens have been lifted!

Praise His name!

Be joyful!

Smile!

Helen Widger Middlebrooke
To Love and to Cherish

Accepting Truth

"Forget about what's happened; don't keep going over old history. Be alert, be present. I'm about to do something brand-new. It's bursting out! Don't you see it? There it is! I'm making a road through the desert, rivers in the badlands."

ISAIAH 43:18–19 MSG

Not only by the grace of God can we accept what is true about our past, but in Christ our very wounds and scars can be redeemed. Pain is hard; there's no doubt. But pain reminds us why Christ died. It reminds us to bring our wounds to the wounded Healer so He can make us better. In turn, we can comfort others as we have been comforted and look to a future free from hurt. We are not asked to pretend our wounds don't exist, but to let go and stop holding on to them so tightly.

Being set free from the past means accepting what is true, not what we wish was true. Sometimes we have to make peace with what was or is to be able to let go and move on. So many of us put ourselves in situations to be hurt over and over by the same person because we know things *should* be different. We cling to our dreams of what we wish the past could have been and set ourselves up to be hurt again and again. If this is you, I encourage you to let go of that past—your "what should have been"—and embrace your "what is" and your "what can be." Truth is powerful. At times it is heartbreaking, but ultimately, it will deliver you.

Sheila Walsh
Let Go

God Speaks

How sweet are your words to my taste,
sweeter than honey to my mouth!
I gain understanding from your precepts;
therefore I hate every wrong path.
Your word is a lamp for my feet,
a light on my path.

PSALM 119:103–105 NIV

After trying for two years to find a publisher for my first book, I desperately needed to hear from God. With tears of frustration, I cried out to Him, "When will all my labor pay off?" He responded through Jeremiah 31:16 (NIV), "'Restrain your voice from weeping and your eyes from tears, for your work will be rewarded,' declares the LORD."

He really heard my cry! And the reward He promised? *Lambs on the Ledge* is now published not only in English, but in Portuguese, Chinese, and Russian, and is being read by pastors and leaders around the world. God is in the midst of every part of your life and mine. He is in the midst of every exciting and fruitful season—but He is also in the midst of the winters when all seems dead and still. He's there as only a best friend can be. And God will speak to us. He will speak through a million images and events around us and through His Word.

As we walk with God, we will be refreshed as we worship, and our souls will be fed as we study His Word. Prayer will become a natural two-way conversation that will give deep direction to our lives.

And God will not disappoint us!

Joyce Strong
Author, Speaker

Experiencing Happily Ever After

So put on all the armor that God gives.
Then when that evil day comes, you will
be able to defend yourself. And when the
battle is over, you will still be standing firm.

EPHESIANS 6:13 CEV

Have you ever noticed that in a fairy tale there's
usually a damsel in distress? She dreams about
the day a valiant knight on his white horse will ride
up to the castle, slay the dragon, use the alligators as
stepping-stones, climb up the tower, and rescue her.

Maybe you've had that dream yourself. Well, stop
dreaming, sister! Your dream has already come true,
and it's heavenly! Your Prince (the Prince of Peace) has
already come on His white horse. And He didn't just
rescue you. He also took away your victim status and
made you into a victor! He even gave you armor—the
full armor of God—to protect you as you fight evil.

Sure, fairy tales are fun to watch on the big screen,
but I don't want to be a damsel in distress in real
life. A princess—yes. A damsel in distress—no. God
doesn't want you to be a damsel in distress, either. If

you've been living with a victim's mentality for too long, it's time to wise up to the Word. The Word says that we can use God's mighty weapons to knock down the devil's strongholds.

Your damsel in distress days are behind you. You are a beautiful princess—a member of God's royal family. And if you've made Jesus the Lord of your life, you are promised an eternity of "happily ever after."

Michelle Medlock Adams
Secrets of Beauty

There's Beauty in Humility

When the turn came for Esther. . .to
go to the king, she asked for nothing
other than what Hegai, the king's
eunuch who was in charge of the harem,
suggested. And Esther won the favor
of everyone who saw her.

ESTHER 2:15 NIV

Imagine a simple Jewish girl, a captive in Persia,
being considered for the position of queen. Esther
knew nothing of palace life in a strange land or how to
please King Xerxes, who held her future in his hands.
Humbly, she recognized her need to rely on others for
wisdom. So Esther looked to the king's harem eunuch,
Hegai, for advice. Hegai must have responded to Esther
wisely, because she not only received the favor of all
who saw her, she won the heart of the king.

No matter what your age or position, at times, you
need advice. Like Esther, do you choose your counsel-
ors wisely? Then do you follow their good advice, or
does pride get in the way?

Humility often requires courage. We assume

people will think poorly of us if we admit we don't know all the facts or the best way to proceed. But often just the opposite is true. Humility has an appeal all its own. Remember, too, people may undervalue this gentle opinion-making quality, but God never will. Perhaps that's why He so often blesses the humble.

Humility doesn't come easily to me, Lord. Help me turn aside from pride and be meek instead.

Pamela L. McQuade
Daily Wisdom for the Workplace

Confident Hope

And Deborah, a prophetess, the wife of
Lapidoth, she judged Israel at that time.

JUDGES 4:4 KJV

Throughout scripture, the faith women had in God
provides them with the confidence to stand up
for their beliefs. One woman is even called to guide
ten thousand men into battle.

The only woman to sit as a judge over Israel,
Deborah already had a strong relationship with the
Lord when she was called to sit as judge for Israel at a
time of harsh oppression. Yet in a society that did not
always value women as leaders, she answered God's
call on her life.

Using her wisdom to settle disputes for her people, however, is a far cry from leading them into battle
against an army featuring nine hundred iron chariots.
Jabin, the king in Canaan, had dealt harshly with the
Israelites for more than twenty years, using his army
to keep them under his rule. Finally, they cried out to
God for relief in what appeared to be an impossible
situation to overcome.

Deborah, however, had the ability to see beyond the current situation. She called on Barak to do as the Lord had commanded, to take his troops and prepare to face Sisera, Jabin's general, in a battle to save their people. Barak's response—that he would do so only if she was with him—underscores the trust Israel had placed in the woman God had called for them.

God looks for women who are ready to embrace His vision. Such women of vision have the courage that enables them to conquer and overcome in situations that would otherwise seem unconquerable.

Ramona Richards
Secrets of Confidence

Failure Misconception

His divine power has given us everything
we need for a godly life through our
knowledge of him who called us by his
own glory and goodness.

2 PETER 1:3 NIV

It is easy to think that one failure marks our identity as a failure. That is what the enemy wants us to believe. If he can make us feel as though we are a failure, then he's the winner.

Failure is just part of life, and the sooner we accept that we are flawed humans who depend on the perfect Christ, the sooner we put the taskmaster of perfection away.

What is failure anyway, except a man-made yard-stick for performance? God is much more interested in the process than the product. If I obey God and lose the sale, I am still a success in God's eyes.

Perhaps it is not failure of a spiritual nature that has you bound. Perhaps it's failure of a marriage, of a job, of simple tasks that have influenced the perception that you are a failure. If so, consider this:

One basketball player missed nine thousand shots in his career. He lost more than three hundred games. Twenty-six times he was trusted to take the game's winning shot and missed. His name is Michael Jordan. He said, "I've failed over and over again in my life. And that's why I succeed."

We need to reject the lie of the enemy who tries to kick us when we are down by telling us the lie. Failure can be the springboard for future success.

Sharon Jaynes
"I'm Not Good Enough"...
and Other Lies Women Tell Themselves

Hope Conquers Fear

And they who know Your name [who
have experience and acquaintance
with Your mercy] will lean on and
confidently put their trust in You,
for You, Lord, have not forsaken those
who seek (inquire of and for) You.

PSALM 9:10 AMP

Fear comes in many sizes, shapes, and forms.

As Christians, how do we face fear?

When fear invades our spirits, we need to turn to
the One in whom we have confidence—Jesus Christ.
The One who tells us that He is with us always, "to the
very end of the age" (Matthew 28:20 NIV).

Although we may not understand why certain
things happen in our lives, God instructs us to be
courageous, for "no one will be able to stand against
you all the days of your life. . . . I will be with you; I
will never leave you nor forsake you" (Joshua 1:5 NIV).
Do you have this confidence—that God is with you in
the storms of life?

David wrote of his trust in God in many of the

Psalms, most notably, Psalm 23: "I will fear no evil, for you are with me" (verse 4 NIV).

The only confidence we have in this life is knowing that God is always with us. And if we are wise enough, we will look for and find God in every moment, filled with the assurance that He is with us through the good and the bad. If we follow God—through prayer and the application of His Word—He will keep us close to Him, traveling down the right path, until we reach our home, where He greets us.

Donna K. Maltese
Power Prayers to Start Your Day

Jesus' Prayers

Christ Jesus who died—more than that,
who was raised to life—is at the right
hand of God and is also interceding for us.

ROMANS 8:34 NIV

Several years ago I visited with an older woman I
knew from childhood. She knew my family and
the difficult dynamics, as well as my husband's family
of origin. My husband had grandparents that prayed
fervently for their children and grandchildren. As we
talked together about my husband and I serving the
Lord, she looked at me and asked, "Jocelyn, I know who
was praying for Bruce. But who was praying for you?"

I left her house but her question remained in my
mind. Several days later as I read Romans 8, the Lord
answered our question. The words hit me like a ton of
bricks: *It was Jesus.*

All those years of aimless wandering, little sense
of purpose and worth, dumb decisions, and pain. He
was the One praying for me the entire time. He was
the One talking to the Father on my behalf, reminding
Him that the price of my sin had been paid. He was

the One asking for mercy, grace, and protection as I stumbled in utter confusion. He was the One who saw and declared the future and hope that lay ahead.

Jesus is praying for us. Be encouraged no matter the circumstance. We have the greatest prayer partner we could ever want. Jesus Christ, King of kings and Lord of lords, is praying for you today.

Jocelyn Hamsher
Circle of Friends

Hope in the Advocate

"And I will ask the Father, and he will give you another advocate to help you and be with you forever—the Spirit of truth."

JOHN 14:16–17 NIV

During Jesus' Last Supper discourse, He reassured the disciples that He would not leave them as orphans. The Greek word here for "advocate," which is also translated *helper* (NASB) and *comforter* (KJV) is *parakletos* and means a "person summoned to one's aid." Originally it was a term used in a court of justice to denote a legal assistant, counsel for the defense, an advocate; then, generally, one who pleads another's cause, an intercessor, an advocate.

I love the image of being in a court of law because I have come to see Satan as the "accuser of our brethren" (Revelation 12:10 NASB). He points his gnarly finger in our faces and says things like, "You aren't a very good Christian," "Jesus doesn't really love you," "You were a mistake when you were born," "You've really blown it this time," "I don't see much fruit in your life," "You're a pitiful excuse as a wife, as a mother, as a child of God." Have you ever heard any of those statements before? Perhaps you've always assumed these were your own musings. I believe those accusatory statements are words from Satan that he whispers in our ears.

On the other hand, the Holy Spirit is our counselor, our attorney, the one who comes alongside us and repeats, "Not guilty! Not guilty! Not guilty!" He says, "You, My child, have been set free! Your debt has been paid in full."

Sharon Jaynes
Becoming a Woman Who Listens to God

Looking Ahead to Where God Is

But Jesus told him, "Anyone who puts
a hand to the plow and then looks back
is not fit for the Kingdom of God."

LUKE 9:62 NLT

We know that we shouldn't worry about tomorrow, but even worse is to worry and feel regret about the past, which can only cripple us for tomorrow. "I wish things could be the way they were." "I wish I were younger." "I wish my husband treated me like he did when we first met." "I wish I could fit into those jeans again. . . ." "I wish, I wish, I wish."

Although the Lord doesn't want us looking back at what once was, our enemy does. He wants us to feel discouraged and helpless over what we face today and drown in self-pity about how it was in the past. But God wants us to look ahead to the future. The future is where He is. He promises to give us hope in our futures. Let's claim that promise for ourselves, for our spouses, and for our marriages. Let's forget the past— it's long gone already and cannot be changed. Let's

move ahead and press toward the new things that the
Lord wants to do in our lives.

Nicole O'Dell
To Love and to Cherish

Never Uncomfortable

My eyes fail, looking for your promise;
I say, "When will you comfort me?"

PSALM 119:82 NIV

Our Comforter is not far off in heaven where we cannot find Him. He is close at hand. He abides with us. When Christ was going away from this earth, He told His disciples that He would not leave them comfortless, but would send "another Comforter" who would abide with them forever. This Comforter, He said, would teach them all things, and would bring all things to their remembrance. And then He declared, as though it were the necessary result of the coming of this divine Comforter: "Peace I leave with you, my peace I give unto you; not as the world giveth, give I unto you. Let not your heart [therefore] be troubled, neither let it be afraid." Oh, how can we, in the face of these tender and loving words, go about with troubled and frightened hearts?

Comforter—what a word of bliss, if we only could realize it. Let us repeat it over and over to ourselves, until its meaning sinks into the very depths of our being. And an "abiding" Comforter, too, not one who comes and goes, and is never on hand when most needed, but one who is always present, and always ready to give us "joy for mourning, the garment of praise for the spirit of heaviness."

If we can have a human comforter to stay with us for only a few days when we are in trouble, we think ourselves fortunate; but here is a divine Comforter who is always staying with us, and whose power to comfort is infinite. Never, never ought we for a single minute to be without comfort; never for a single minute ought we to be uncomfortable.

Hannah Whitall Smith
The God of All Comfort

For Us Who Believe

I pray that the eyes of your heart may be
enlightened in order that you may know
the hope to which he has called you, the
riches of his glorious inheritance in his
holy people, and his incomparably great
power for us who believe.

EPHESIANS 1:18–19 NIV

No matter what you're facing today—no matter what giants are standing in your path—if God gives you the vision, He will give you the provision. He doesn't necessarily call the equipped, but He always equips the called. You have what it takes. God has given you the power of the Holy Spirit. That same power is what transformed Peter from a coward who denied he even knew Jesus into a courageous leader who spoke out with confidence and passion after Jesus' ascension.

Satan wants us to believe that we don't have what it takes. God's truth is that we have everything we need. The power of the Holy Spirit has been given to us, is living in us, and is working through us. But here's the key. That power is *for those who believe* (Ephesians 1:18–20). The power is available, but we must believe to receive.

Satan tells me, "You can't."

God tells me, "I already have."

The only obstacle keeping us from doing all that God has called us to do and being all that God has called us to be is our unbelief. It was the same with the Israelites headed to the Promised Land, and it's the same for you and me headed to ours. Jesus said, "All things are possible to those who believe."

Sharon Jaynes
"I'm Not Good Enough". . . and
Other Lies Women Tell Themselves

Hope in the Truth

But if we walk in the light, as he is in
the light, we have fellowship with
one another, and the blood of Jesus,
his Son, purifies us from all sin.

1 JOHN 1:7 NIV

As a child, I suffered a crippling fear of the dark.
Monsters crouched under my bed and in the
closet. Only a wedge of light from the living room
held them at bay, along with my nightly ritual recitation of the Lord's Prayer. Another terrifying door led
from my bedroom to the hundred-and-fifty-year-old
stone basement in our small house. From the age of
six, I practiced locking it tightly before going to bed.

Other fears held me fast, too, things I didn't talk
about. With my father's mental illness and disappearance when I was seven, followed by his death a few
years later, death became my greatest fear of all; not
my own, but the horrible fear that my mother or older
brother might die as well.

As I became an adult, I found that fears don't go
away. They just change masks and whisper low growling

threats from their hiding place. What if my child dies? Or my husband? Does God care about me? Is He even real?

He heard.

There came a day, bright as the morning, when new friends grasped my hand and walked me toward the Light. With their help, I placed my trust in Jesus, the Truth I'd long sought, the Way to my real Father, God. In His presence darkness cannot exist, fear loses its death grip, and His forever Love set me free.

Virelle Kidder
The Best Life Ain't Easy, But It's Worth It

Joy in the Morning

The LORD is close to the brokenhearted
and saves those who are crushed in spirit.

PSALM 34:18 NIV

Joy, a mother of three, struggled silently with her
pains of loneliness and discouragement. No one
really knew how desperate she felt. When she risked
sharing, it was generally met with an endearing soul
trying to assure her, "It will get better." But the truth
was she was barely holding on—trying to make it
through another day, another restless night.

She was waiting for things to change, waiting for
someone to come to her aid or the dawn of a new day
that would bring a new reality. She was tired of hopes
and dreams. She had been there and done that, but the
grim realities remained. Her life was mundane and
full of recurring hurts from careless words, lack of
appreciation, and unfulfilled dreams. Her energy was
gone. She was putting on a mask, welcoming everyone
with a cheerful hello and smile. Hope was gone. She
felt overwhelmed, underappreciated, and extremely
unhappy.

It is easy to become self-absorbed when life isn't going the way you want. It is also easy to judge others for not understanding, not being there for you, or not being able to "fix" your problem.

He is close to the brokenhearted, those who are at the end of their rope. He offers understanding that has no limits, healing for every wound, and mighty power to enable you to stand firm through the tough time until once again your heart can experience joy in the morning and throughout your day.

Bobbie Rill
Family Life Radio Network

The Dance of the Delighted

"The LORD your God is with you,
the Mighty Warrior who saves.
He will take great delight in you,
in his love he will no longer rebuke you,
but will rejoice over you with singing."

ZEPHANIAH 3:17 NIV

M y youngest nephew, who is seven, is mad about
guinea pigs. I spent one evening hanging out
with John Michael while he frolicked with his furry
friends. He danced in circles around them, "chatted"
nose to nose with them, and stretched out on the floor
so the pseudorats could scurry around on his tummy.
The entire time, he kept erupting into contagious
giggles!

My nephew wasn't doing anything particularly
praiseworthy, he was simply doing what he loves
to do. It's taken me a very long time to believe that
God delights in me, even when I'm just being me.
I used to think God was a stern taskmaster and the
only time He was pleased with me was when I was
doing something "religious," like volunteering with

children's Sunday school or teaching the Bible at a women's conference. Basically I thought He loved me out of duty—because it was written in His divine job description. The concept of God's delighting in me seemed as plausible as pigs flying.

But this petite book named after a minor prophet actually records that eye-popping promise. Even though God's people were behaving badly, even though they deserved a big fat spanking, our merciful Creator chose to sing lyrics of restoration. Instead of knocking them across the room, He crooned a love song. And that kind of music makes me feel like dancing!

Lisa Harper
What the Bible Is All About for Women

No Outlet

Commit thy way unto the LORD; trust
also in him; and he shall bring it to pass.

PSALM 37:5 KJV

We can learn to live with difficult circumstances.
Grace has the power to turn a seeming dead
end into a new beginning, one that sets us on the path
to life without end, amen. It is in that divine moment
when grace breaks through the impossible situation
and sets us emotionally free that we grow in our love
for God. The reality of eternity is painted against the
backdrop of our broken, hurting lives.

Sometimes, while traveling on life's journey, we
get stopped by a bad attitude or sin, which can cripple
us. We must first pull over and admit that something
in our lives needs to change. Then we must jack the
wheel off the ground and lift that situation to God in
prayer. After that, we must remove the flat tire and
replace it with a new one, substituting the wrong
attitude with a positive one.

When we make a commitment to fill our hearts
with thoughts of His grace and power, the breath of

God can inflate our flattened view of life. The word *encourage* means "to fill the heart." Encouragement can actually inflate a deflated attitude because it fills us with hope.

What is hope? It is the conviction that, despite all the black around you, despite the fact that you see no sign of an exit, you will find a way out—with God's help.

Barbara Johnson
The Joyful Journey

I Have Planned Ahead for You

Nevertheless I am continually with You;
You have taken hold of my right hand.
With Your counsel You will guide me.

PSALM 73:23–24 NASB

Behold, am I a God that is afar off, and not a God that is near? For in the midst of difficulties, I will be your support. In the darkness, I am your Light; there is no darkness that can hide My face from the eye of faith. My beauty and My radiance are all the lovelier in darkness.

In grief, My comfort is more poignant. In failure, My encouragement the most welcome. In loneliness, the touch of My presence more tender. You are hidden in Me, and I will multiply both the wisdom and the strength in due proportion to meet the demands of every occasion.

I am the Lord your God. I know no limitations. I know no lack. I need not reserve My stores, for I always have a fresh supply. You can by no means ever exhaust My infinite resources. Let your heart run wild. Let your imagination go vagabond. No extravagance of human thought can ever plumb the depths of My planning and provision for My children.

Rejoice, therefore, and face each day with joy; for I have planned ahead for you and made all necessary arrangements and reservations. I am your guide and benefactor. Put your hand in Mine.

Frances J. Roberts
Come Away My Beloved

Acting in Love

"I—yes, I alone—will blot out
your sins for my own sake and
will never think of them again."

ISAIAH 43:25 NLT

Our awe-inspiring God demands perfection, and we so rarely give Him anything barely resembling it. When we look at our own imperfection, it's easy to become discouraged. Can we ever hit the mark? When we feel that way, we're much like a child who has disappointed Father. We respond with fear, doubt, or even resentment because we've made a mistake or intentionally disobeyed.

Before negative emotion gains ground in our lives, we must realize that God never loves us because we act perfectly any more than we want to give our children that kind of conditional love. God blots out sin not because of our character, but because of His. He wants to love us so badly that even sending Jesus to die for us was not too great a price.

Discouraged by your own sinfulness? Don't give up—give it to God. He'll forgive your past wrongs and forget them all as He gives you strength for new life in Him.

Forgive me, Lord, the wrongs I've done and the attitudes that do not glorify You. Change my heart and soul and make me whole in You.

Pamela L. McQuade
Daily Wisdom for the Workplace

Choose Faith

Don't be afraid, because I am your God.
I will make you strong and will help you;
I will support you with my right hand
that saves you.

ISAIAH 41:10 NCV

I have never met a woman who has not struggled at
some level with the fear of success or the fear of
failure. One woman wrote, "I have desperately wanted
everyone, anyone, or someone to think I was wonderful, talented, exciting, and spiritual." This woman's
self-esteem was so fragile due to past issues that she
was in bondage to the fear of failure.

On the other hand, some of us are overwhelmed
by the secret fear that to be successful, we must do
something so spectacular that the whole world will
validate our worth. When we get caught up in this
philosophy, we often do accomplish something worthy
of applause, but often the fear of failure looms in the
background because of the personal sacrifices that
have allowed the success.

Much of our fear centers on being unable to

identify what will bring a sense of purpose, joy, and fulfillment to our lives. Fear of making the wrong choice in our life's work. Fear of getting trapped in dead-end marriages and/or vocations. Fear of not having children. Fear of having children and being bad parents. Fear of trying something new because we've never succeeded in the past.

The opposite of fear is faith. Fear makes us withdraw and hide behind our escape mechanisms. Fear exposes our disappointments and makes us choose a rigid or a yielding resolution for those fears. Faith or fear? The choice is ours.

Carol Kent
Tame Your Fears

Worry or Worship

"Therefore do not worry about tomorrow, for tomorrow will worry about its own things. Sufficient for the day is its own trouble."

MATTHEW 6:34 NKJV

It is when we find ourselves in these hard places that we make the choice to worry or worship. When we worry, we feel we have to come up with justifications and careful explanations for the naysayers. When we worry, we listen to the voices of Acceptance and Rejection. When we worry, we lay awake at night and ponder Satan's lies. When we worry, we have pity parties where the guests of honor are Negative Thinking, Doubt, and Resignation.

But we can make the choice to worship. When we worship in these hard places, we are reminded that none of this is about us—it is all about God. We turn our focus off of ourselves and back onto God Almighty. God can use empty places in your life to draw your heart to Him. He is the great love of your life who will never disappoint. He is building your eternal home that will never get broken, dirty, or need redecorating. He is preparing a place of eternal perfect fellowship.

We all worship something. We must choose whom—or what—we will worship. Will it be the opinions of others, our fears, or even our own comfort? Or will it be the One who created our souls to worship? Whatever we worship, we will obey. As we choose to be radically obedient to the Lord, we must be radical about choosing to worship Him and Him alone.

Lysa TerKeurst
Radically Obedient, Radically Blessed

Heaven Is No Dream

Thy mercy, O LORD, is in the heavens; and thy faithfulness reacheth unto the clouds.

PSALM 36:5 KJV

This evening the clouds lay low on the mountains, so that sometimes we could hardly see them, and sometimes the stars were nearly all covered. But always, just when it seemed as though the mountains were going to be quite lost in the mist, the higher peaks pushed out, and whereas the dimmer stars were veiled, the brighter ones shone through. Even supposing the clouds had wholly covered the face of the mountains and not a star had shone through the piled-up masses, the mountains would still have stood steadfast, and the stars would not have ceased to shine.

I thought of this and found it very comforting, simple as it is. Our feelings do not affect God's facts. They may blow up like clouds and cover the eternal things that we do most truly believe. We may not see the shining of the promises, but still they shine; and the strength of the hills that is His also, is not for one moment less because of our human weakness.

Heaven is no dream. Feelings go and come like clouds, but the hills and the stars abide.

Amy Carmichael
Edges of His Ways

The River

Consider it pure joy. . .whenever
you face trials of many kinds.

JAMES 1:2 NIV

Finding joy in the trials of life is like finding a precious stone embedded along a river's edge. As the water rages on, it is almost impossible to spot the stone's vibrant colors, but when the water is still, it is easy to see how it's been there all along. These are deep lessons that, when gathered together, strengthen our faith.

Turning away from trials is our natural response to life, but if we remember the river and the treasures that await us, they become easier to bear. Jesus tells us that throughout life we will have many troubles. At the same time, He offers us strength by reminding us that He has overcome them all (John 16:33). This is of great comfort to us when life becomes the raging river, and we struggle just to keep our head above the water.

In time, as the water of our days ebbs and flows, eventually the turbulence passes. We gasp and cough and cling to shore to find we survived, not only the current that threatened to pull us under, but our own doubt as well. And blinking to us in the sunlight, caught along the riverbank, are pearls of wisdom and a jewel called hope.

Sarah Hawkins
To Love and to Cherish

Death Conqueror

"The thief does not come except to
steal, and to kill, and to destroy. I have
come that they may have life, and that
they may have it more abundantly."

JOHN 10:10 NKJV

When Jesus died on the cross, He also rose
from the dead to break the power of death
over anyone who receives His life. Jesus conquered
death—whether at the end of our lives or in the
multiple ways that we face death daily. In the death of
our dreams, finances, health, or relationships, Jesus
can bring His life to resurrect those dead places in us.
Therefore we don't have to feel hopeless.

He also gives to everyone who opens up to Him a
quality of life that is meaningful, abundant, and fulfilling. He transcends our every limitation and boundary
and enables us to do things we never would have been
capable of aside from Him. He is the only one with
power and authority over the emotions or bondage
that torture us. He is the only one who can give us life

before death as well as life hereafter.

Without Him we die a little every day. With Him we become more and more alive.

Stormie Omartian
Praying God's Will for Your Life

Sincere Faith

But we have this treasure in jars of clay to show that this all-surpassing power is from God and not from us.

2 CORINTHIANS 4:7 NIV

I firmly believe the world doesn't need to see how perfect we are; it needs to see how powerful God is. People don't need to see how Christians never have any problems and never make any mistakes; they need to see how God is bigger than our problems and more powerful than our mistakes.

Another of my favorite passages is 2 Corinthians 2:17 (NIV): "Unlike so many, we do not peddle the word of God for profit. On the contrary, in Christ we speak before God with sincerity, as those sent from God."

In the original Greek, the word *sincerity*, or sincere faith, literally means "without wax." During New Testament times, clay pots were big business. They were like first-century Tupperware—used for hauling and storing everything imaginable. Each jar of clay was handmade, and it was inevitable that there would be some kind of crack or flaw somewhere in it. Everyone knew about the cracks. But since it was big business, the people selling the clay pots would cover the cracks with wax. It was all a game.

In the same way, we have this treasure—the radiance and glory of the living God—but we have it in a jar of clay. Each of us is handmade by God, completely unique. But since we live in a fallen world, where our fellow jars of clay routinely bump into us, some cracks are inevitable.

Donna Partow
This Isn't the Life I Signed Up For

Quiet Beauty

Let it be the hidden person of the
heart, with the incorruptible beauty
of a gentle and quiet spirit, which
is very precious in the sight of God.

1 PETER 3:4 NKJV

Silver-haired and sixtyish, Elizabeth radiated stylish
poise and unflappable acceptance of others. Her
husband, Fred, was a quiet man, likeable but not much
for socializing. Whenever he came to church, they
amazed me by often holding hands, and I'd think to
myself, *That's the kind of marriage I wish we could have
someday*.

One day I confided my deep loneliness at home and
the terrible longing I felt for Steve to share my faith.

"I know how you feel, Virelle," she answered, level-
ing those beautiful gray-blue eyes at me. "I've been
praying for Fred for forty years."

"What?" I blurted out my amazement. "How have
you lasted that long? How come you both seem so
happy?"

"I learned one day that God called me to love

Fred, to honor him, and make his life as happy as I possibly could. He never asked me to change him. Only someone as big and as powerful as God can change a husband!"

And He did. I learned many years later that Fred received Christ as Savior shortly before his death. What made Elizabeth so beautiful? It had to be her loving heart, one that ruled her tongue, her facial expressions, her voice, her touch, her time. She was the evidence I needed, the perfect visual of a Christ-filled life. I wanted to become like that, no matter what it took.

Virelle Kidder
The Best Life Ain't Easy, But It's Worth It

Just as You Are

"But while he was still a long way off, his father saw him and was filled with compassion for him; he ran to his son, threw his arms around him and kissed him."

LUKE 15:20 NIV

As we went around the table, I listened to the women each share who they were, what they did, and some struggles they face in their job. I knew immediately I did not belong. After I took my turn, I had every woman looking at me as if I had four ears growing out of my head. There was an awkward silence, and then we moved on to the next lady. The catch phrase "Wanna get away?" echoed in my mind.

Scripture continually paints God as our Father who wants us to come to Him as we are. He doesn't want us to pretend we are someone we are not. He doesn't expect us or require us to have it all together. Jesus called disciples who were not considered "smart" enough by Jewish teachers to follow and learn from Him. He beckoned others who were hated and treated as outcasts. He showed love and gave value to women who in society's eyes deserved to die. His ancestors consisted of the righteous and sinners alike—adulterers, prostitutes, and those from dysfunctional families. Jesus wants us as we are—despite our past mistakes, present struggles, or fears for the future. He wants us no matter how long we have been away. He is waiting with arms open wide. God wants us to come to Him, to be a part of His family.

Jocelyn Hamsher
Circle of Friends

Hope for Unanswered Questions

Why are you in despair, O my soul? And
why have you become disturbed within me?
Hope in God, for I shall yet praise Him,
the help of my countenance and my God.

PSALM 42:11 NASB

No matter what the pain and problems may be like, everybody is looking for the answers to two basic questions: Why? and How? Folks who write to me often ask, "Why me?" "Why us?" "Why our family?" But just as often they also want to know, "How?" "How can I deal with this?" "How do I learn to live with pain?"

I don't have all the answers. Frankly, sometimes I'm not even sure I fully understand the questions. I wish I could always have something to say that would make everything all right, right now, but I don't. I do know one thing, though:

Whatever comes to any of us
is sent or allowed by God.

To some people, that may make God sound weak, uncaring, or even sadistic, but when you're facing the real world it helps to remember that God is in control. He is still at work, even when we feel that our suffering will never end. Like the psalmist commanded, we must "hope. . .in God" (Psalm 42:5 KJV).

Barbara Johnson
The Best of Barbara Johnson

Don't Miss It!

And we know that in all things
God works for the good of those
who love him, who have been
called according to his purpose.

ROMANS 8:28 NIV

That good could be knowing God more intimately, being conformed to the image of Christ more completely, understanding the scriptures more clearly, communing with the Spirit more intimately, falling in love with Him more dearly. God often allows or orchestrates certain circumstances in our lives in order to draw us into dependency on Him and intimacy with Him.

All day long God is working in and around us. It is so easy to simply go about the task of living without seeing God's handprints on our circumstances and footprints on our paths. When we see life as a to-do list to check off or random acts of fortune to celebrate or misfortune to endure, we will miss seeing God and hearing His voice as the scarlet thread that connects the moments and the days of our lives.

It is so easy to miss God speaking through our circumstances. Jesus' first miracle occurred at a wedding in Cana. Some noticed the miracle and some did not. Sometimes God speaks to us in very unlikely ways, and if we're not looking for it, we may miss it. Being in tune with His voice requires more than our ears to hear and our eyes to see. Oh, how I never want to miss God working through my circumstances as I travel through life!

Sharon Jaynes
Becoming a Woman Who Listens to God

Find Your True Self

"Naked I came from my mother's
womb, and naked I will depart.
The LORD gave and the LORD
has taken away; may the name
of the LORD be praised."

JOB 1:21 NIV

There is no ongoing spiritual life without this process of letting go. At the precise point where we refuse, growth stops. If we hold tightly to anything given to us, unwilling to let it go when the time comes to let it go or unwilling to allow it to be used as the Giver means it to be used, we stunt the growth of the soul.

It is easy to make a mistake here. "If God gave it to me," we say, "it's mine. I can do what I want with it." No. The truth is that it is ours to thank Him for and ours to offer back to Him, ours to relinquish, ours to lose, ours to let go of—if we want to find our true selves, if we want real life, if our hearts are set on glory.

Elisabeth Elliot
Passion and Purity

Guidance

"I'll take the hand of those who don't know the way, who can't see where they're going. I'll be a personal guide to them, directing them through unknown country. I'll be right there to show them what roads to take, make sure they don't fall into the ditch. These are the things I'll be doing for them—sticking with them, not leaving them for a minute."

ISAIAH 42:16 MSG

The guidance of the Spirit is generally by gentle suggestions or drawings, not in violent pushes; it requires great childlikeness of heart to be faithful to it. The secret of being made willing lies in a definite giving up of our will.

You must lay this burden about any service to which you may be called wholly upon your burden bearer. If He wants you to do it, He will supply all the needed strength and wisdom, and you don't even have to think of it or worry about it for one single moment. Only see to it that you yield yourself up to Him perfectly, and then leave it with Him. There never must be any indulgence in an unsurrendered will in any respect, for this would bring darkness at once.

Now you must claim continually that it is true. When it seems to be the most untrue, then claim and assert it with the greatest boldness. This is what it means to lift up the shield of faith, and this is the way to overcome by faith. It is marvelous to see what He can do with even the poorest and the weakest instruments that are pliable in His hands!

Hannah Whitall Smith
The Christian's Secret of a Holy Life

Sweet Deliverance

She said to herself, "If I only
touch his cloak, I will be healed."

MATTHEW 9:21 NIV

O My child, I am coming to thee walking upon
the waters of the sorrows of thy life; yea, above
the sounds of the storm ye shall hear My voice calling
thy name.

Ye are never alone, for I am at thy right hand.
Never despair, for I am watching over and caring for
thee. Be not anxious. What seemeth to thee to be at
present a difficult situation is all part of My planning,
and I am working out the details of circumstances to
the end that I may bless thee and reveal Myself to thee
in a new way.

As I have opened thine eyes to see, so shall I open
thine ears to hear, and ye shall come to know Me even
as did Moses, yea, in a face-to-face relationship.

For I shall remove the veil that separates Me from
thee and ye shall know Me as thy dearest Friend and as
thy truest Comforter.

No darkness shall hide the shining of My face, for I

shall be to thee as a bright star in the night sky. Never let thy faith waver. Reach out thy hand, and thou shalt touch the hem of My garment.

Frances J. Roberts
Come Away My Beloved

The World's First GPS System

Then the angel of God, who had been traveling in front of Israel's army, withdrew and went behind them. The pillar of cloud also moved from in front and stood behind them, coming between the armies of Egypt and Israel. Throughout the night the cloud brought darkness to the one side and light to the other side; so neither went near the other all night long.

EXODUS 14:19–20 NIV

The world's first known GPS system was the pillar of cloud by day or fire by night that led the Israelites through the Sinai Peninsula. Imagine how comforting it was for the Israelites to follow that pillar on their trek. Better than a road map! It was a visible symbol, concrete evidence, of the presence of God.

Imagine if we had that holy pillar outside of our front door to help us with big decisions: *Lord, should we take that job and move to another state? Or should we just stay put?*

We do have that holy pillar outside of our homes.

Inside, too. The Bible! Searching God's Word is like choosing to follow a map in a new country. He shows us where we need to end up and how we need to get there. Like God's people crossing the barren Sinai desert, the Bible teaches us to listen for God's directions, whether it's "Stop!" or "Camp here tonight" or "Quick, get a move on!" or "Time to rest." God's voice in our ear is the only map we need.

Suzanne Woods Fisher

To Love and to Cherish

Light at the End of the Tunnel

The people who walk in darkness will
see a great light. For those who live in a
land of deep darkness, a light will shine.

ISAIAH 9:2 NLT

Are you in need of a glimmer of light at the end of the tunnel? Isaiah promises that even in darkness, even in death itself, there is good ground for hope. The power of God is able to restore life to His people even when they appear already dead!

What is that great light? It is the Savior, Jesus Christ. This prediction was fulfilled by Christ's coming (Matthew 4:16). The light of Christ brought the promise of deliverance for Israel. A new day had come!

The Savior is a great light in the darkness to us as well. Maybe you live in the darkness of divorce or in the shadow of death. Some of you may be watching a loved one slowly disintegrate before your eyes. Perhaps you have given up seeing any light in a dark family or church situation. Others, in seemingly perfect circumstances, live in the deepest darkness of all—depression that nothing seems to penetrate! Listen to the Good News!

There's light at the end of the tunnel—look up and see Jesus standing there! Hear what He says: "I am the light of the world. If you follow me, you won't have to walk in darkness, because you will have the light that leads to life" (John 8:12 NLT).

The Word of God penetrates the darkness of our soul. It's as if God penetrates the darkness with His inescapable light. Ask God to penetrate your tunnel of darkness with His glorious light.

Jill Briscoe
The One Year Book of Devotions for Women

Righteousness for Ragamuffins

For He made Him who knew no sin to
be sin for us, that we might become
the righteousness of God in Him.

2 CORINTHIANS 5:21 NKJV

My smart but spacey friend enthused in a strong
Southern twang, "You know, I think the Gospel
is kind of like the Cinderella story. Christians are like
Cinderella and Jesus is like the prince."

After mulling it over for a while, I realized the
reason I had such a strong aversion to the analogy was
because Cinderella deserved the prince. If you've read
the book or watched the DVD, you probably remember
that Cinderella was beautiful. She was also a friend of
animals and had an admirable work ethic. So when the
slipper fits and the prince confesses his crush, most of
us sigh dreamily, grateful for the happy ending—glad
the good girl ends up with the good guy.

That is so not the Gospel.

In God's story, the prince falls head over heels in love
with the ugly stepsister—the one with moles on her
face, frizzy hair, a whiny personality, and elastic-waist

pants. She isn't pretty, inside or out. The whole ballroom lets out a collective gasp when the handsome prince strides across the floor and asks her to dance. His choice in partners doesn't make sense. She doesn't deserve His affection, or anyone else's for that matter.

Then something amazing happens: as she's enveloped in the prince's adoring embrace, the stepsister becomes beautiful.

That's the Gospel.

Lisa Harper
What the Bible Is All About for Women

Unfailing Love

Every good and perfect gift is
from above, coming down from the
Father of the heavenly lights, who
does not change like shifting shadows.

JAMES 1:17 NIV

God is not moody, loving us one day and raging against us the next. He does not change His good intentions toward us. Daily He extends new mercies and looks for our open hands, into which He wants to deposit invaluable, immeasurable blessings. He is always faithful to deliver on His promises.

We tend to be suspicious of God because we see Him through the haze of what our own hearts are capable of. *We* change our minds. *We* feel stingy or generous on any given day depending on how others treat us. *We* are reserved with others based on past hurts and disappointments.

But His ways are not our ways. His thoughts are not our thoughts. God keeps short accounts. He does not superimpose the past over the future. He is able to let bygones be bygones. So no matter what you have done, He is ready to start anew. He's ready to start blessing you all over again.

Don't you just love that about Him?

Michelle McKinney Hammond
How to Be Blessed and Highly Favored

Confidence to Serve Well

[Deborah] held court under the Palm of Deborah. . .and the Israelites went up to her to have their disputes decided.

JUDGES 4:5 NIV

What an unusual person Deborah was! Judges were usually men, yet she held this position of importance, deciding major issues for the people of Israel. In a time when most people thought of women as being fairly unimportant, she held a powerful position and seems to have been a good leader.

Like Deborah, we can find ourselves in unusual jobs. Perhaps you're the only person of your sex on your job. Maybe you are young, working with people greatly senior to you. Or perhaps you are the only person of your race on the job. Being the one who's different can be a challenge. Your position can be one to complain about or one to learn from. The scriptures don't show Deborah whining or complaining. She took charge of the situation. She did her best for God, and an impressive best it was.

Whether you fit in completely or find yourself in

a tough spot, you're there to serve God, not complain or quit easily. So make even your differences work for God, no matter what they are.

I may feel different, Lord, but You've given me this place. Let me serve You by doing my best every day.

Pamela L. McQuade
Daily Wisdom for the Workplace

Making Payments

"If any of you wants to be my follower,
you must turn from your selfish ways,
take up your cross daily, and follow
me. If you try to hang on to your life,
you will lose it. But if you give up
your life for my sake, you will save it."

LUKE 9:23–24 NLT

When you buy a house you first make a large
down payment. Then, to keep the house, you
must make a smaller payment every time it comes
due. You can't change your mind and say, "I don't feel
like making payments!" without serious consequences.

The same is true of your relationship with God. To
make Him your permanent dwelling place, your initial
down payment consists of making Him Lord over
your life. After that, ongoing payments must be made,
which means saying yes whenever God directs you
to do something. They are all a part of the purchase,
but one happens initially and the other is eternally
ongoing (just like house payments!). The difference is
that the Lord will take only as much payment from me

as I am willing to give Him. And I can possess only as much of what He has for me as I am willing to secure with my obedience.

Stormie Omartian
Praying God's Will for Your Life

Eternal Perspective

Simon Peter answered him, "Lord, who would we go to? You have the words that give eternal life. We believe and know that you are the Holy One from God."

JOHN 6:68–69 NCV

The account in John 6 says that people were following Jesus. The contrasts in that crowd tell the whole story. They were seeking a circus. Jesus was offering truth. They demanded outward drama. Jesus sought inward change. They looked for a hero. Jesus came to be a servant. When they did not get what they wanted, many of those brand-new disciples packed up their marbles and went home.

Peter went on to deny Jesus three times—but over time his early conviction took root. If we look closely, Peter gives us the secret of an eternal perspective. He reminds us of two important builders: (1) our hope rests in the power of Christ's resurrection; (2) our hope is fixed on the promise of our reward.

No matter what life dishes out along the way, there is nowhere to go but to Christ. Peter's entire challenge to

people in pain involved reminding them they were pilgrims—people who were just passing through this fallen
world. Then he helped them focus on "goin' home."

Think of it. One day doubts and fears will all be
in the past. We will be in a kingdom that cannot be
shaken. No more unanswerable questions. No more
unexplainable suffering. No more riveting doubts. No
more paralyzing fear. We will see Him as He is. As we
look at the nail prints, we will finally understand.

Carol Kent
Tame Your Fears

Mighty Sermons

When Jesus saw his ministry drawing
huge crowds, he climbed a hillside.
Those who were apprenticed to him,
the committed, climbed with him.
Arriving at a quiet place, he sat down
and taught his climbing companions.

MATTHEW 5:1–2 MSG

The unique illustrations given by Dr. Talmage always interested me, one of them in particular. In a Christmas sermon he told the story of a little Swiss girl who was dying; and from her window she could look out to the lofty summit of the mountains amid which she had been reared. "Papa, carry me to the tip of the mountain," she exclaimed. But he replied, "My child, I cannot carry you, but the angels will." For a time she was silent and lay with her eyes closed. At length she opened them and looking out of the window exclaimed in her joy, "They *are* carrying me, father. I shall soon be at the top." With those words Dr. Talmage concluded his sermon. It seemed to his hearers that he had conducted them to a high pinnacle in a lofty range of mountains where they might breathe a pure atmosphere. When I reminded him of the beautiful effect that his words had upon us, he said, "Ah, you are right. I never intended to bring you down from that summit."

And thus it is with even the humblest fellow-ministers; they take us to heights of which the soul often dreams, yet rarely attains, in fact to those mansions of the blest where there are always light and warmth and love; where the thirst of weary pilgrims is quenched by drafts of mountain springs; and where this mortal spirit puts on its immortality.

Fanny Crosby
Memories of Eighty Years

Call on My Name

"They will call on my name and
I will answer them; I will say,
'They are my people,' and they will say,
'The LORD is our God.'"

ZECHARIAH 13:9 NIV

One of the reasons we do not have the whole-ness, fulfillment, and peace we desire is that we have not acknowledged God as the answer to our every need. We think, *He may have given me eternal life, but I don't know if He can handle my financial problems.* Or we think, *I know He can lead me to a better job, but I'm not sure if He can mend this marriage.* Or, *He healed my back, but I don't know if He can take away my depres-sion.* The truth is, He is everything we need, and we have to remember that always. In fact, it's good to tell yourself daily, "God is everything I need," and then say the name of the Lord that answers your specific need at that moment.

Do you need hope? He is called our Hope. Pray, "Jesus, You are my Hope."

Are you weak? He is called our Strength. Pray,

"Jesus, You are my Strength."

Do you need advice? He is called Counselor. Pray, "Jesus, You are my Counselor."

Do you feel oppressed? He is called Deliverer.

Are you lonely? He is called Companion and Friend.

He is also called Immanuel, which means "God with us." He is not some distant, cold being with no interest in you. He is Immanuel, the God who is with you right now to the degree that you acknowledge Him in your life.

Stormie Omartian
Praying God's Will for Your Life

Loving Purpose

"With God all things are possible."

MATTHEW 19:26 NIV

It is almost impossible to estimate the power of purpose in life. Things thought out of reason have been accomplished through purpose. Kingdoms have been torn down and built again, heathen customs have been uprooted and the light of Christianity put in their places, men born under the bondage of hard and unfavorable circumstances have risen above their environments and been powers in the world, the mysteries of the earth and sky have been sought out and their power put to work for mankind, yes, every great and noble deed that has ever been done has had for its captain and soldiers men and women of strong purpose.

I once read of a woman upon a lonely ranch in a foreign land. Her husband had to go away for a week or more, leaving her alone for that time with her little children. He had not been gone long before she was bitten by a poisonous serpent, and she knew that in a few hours, not more than eight, she must die. She remembered her children and that if they were to be kept safe she must in the time left her draw enough water and bake enough bread to supply them until their father returned, or he might find his family all dead. So she worked and prayed that day, sick, fainting, almost unconscious, but love set her purpose strong, and she struggled on. Night came, and her hours were nearly up. She put her babes to bed and wandered out of sight of the cabin to die, but with a determination to live as long as possible for her children's sake. And, morning found her still alive, still walking, and her system beginning to clear from the poison. She lived to tell the story, a monument to the power of a loving purpose.

Mabel Hale
Beautiful Girlhood

What Does God See?

"Since you were precious in My sight,
You have been honored,
And I have loved you."

ISAIAH 43:4 NKJV

If you are disappointed in yourself, you assume God is, too. If your parents discovered when they visited you in college that you had a beer in your fridge and were verbally disappointed, didn't you think God felt that way, too? If you missed a few Sundays at church and bumped into someone in a coffee shop who commented on your absence, didn't you also feel you had let God down? If your child's lowest grade at school was Bible class, didn't you wonder what you had done wrong as a parent and if God considered you a dunderhead? The negatives we receive from others we project onto God, and we walk through our lives thinking we have let Him down and He is very disappointed.

The fact is we're wrong. Jesus told us flat out that's not how our Father thinks. The Gospels are full of stories of Jesus taking the morality of the day and turning it on its head. Jesus never minimized sin, but

He separated the sinner from the sin that had a hold on her. This means He might not like what you do, but He absolutely, unconditionally adores you yourself.

Sheila Walsh
Let Go

Does He Forget Me?

Why, my soul, are you downcast?
Why so disturbed within me?
Put your hope in God, for I will yet
praise him, my Savior and my God.

PSALM 42:11 NIV

Sometimes I experienced moments of great despair. I remember one night when I was outside the barracks on my way to roll call. The stars were beautiful. I remember saying, "Lord, You guide all those stars. You have not forgotten them but You have forgotten Betsie and me."

Then Betsie said, "No, He has not forgotten us. I know that from the Bible. The Lord Jesus said, 'I am with you always, until the end of the world,' and Corrie, He is here with us. We must believe that. It is not what we are *feeling* that counts, but what we believe!"

Feelings come and feelings go
And feelings are deceiving.
My warrant is the Word of God,
None else is worth believing.

I slowly learned not to trust in myself or my faith or my feelings, but to trust in Him. Feelings come and go—they are deceitful. In all that hell around us, the promises from the Bible kept us sane.

Corrie ten Boom

Jesus Is Victor

God of Hope

I pray that God, the source of hope,
will fill you completely with joy and
peace because you trust in him. Then
you will overflow with confident hope
through the power of the Holy Spirit.

ROMANS 15:13 NLT

In our busy, fast-paced lives, we may feel exhausted
at times. Our culture fosters frenzy and ignores the
need for rest and restoration. Constantly putting out
fires and completing tasks, working incessantly, we
may feel discouraged and disheartened with life. There
is more to life than this, isn't there?

Our God of hope says, "Yes!" God desires to fill
us to the brim with joy and peace. But to receive this
gladness, rest, and tranquility, we need to have faith in
the God who is trustworthy and who says, "Anything
is possible if a person believes" (Mark 9:23 NLT). We
need to place our confidence in God who, in His timing
and through us, will complete that task, mend that
relationship, or do whatever it is we need. The key
to receiving and living a life of hope, joy, and peace is

recounting God's faithfulness out loud, quietly in your heart, and to others. When you begin to feel discouraged, exhausted, and at the end of your rope, stop; go before the throne of grace and recall God's faithfulness.

Tina C. Elacqua
Whispers of Wisdom for Busy Women

A Test of Faith

The LORD will vindicate me;
your love, LORD, endures forever—
do not abandon the works of your hands.

PSALM 138:8 NIV

At some point in our lives, most of us will face a faith test. It is in that moment in time when what we have always believed about who God is and what He allows to happen in our lives intersects with the reality of our experiences—a head-on collision between our faith and the hard facts of an impossible situation. It's a time when we sometimes question the goodness of God because we are having difficulty understanding what "trust" looks like. On the surface, nothing makes sense. We relive the scene of an accident or we remember the details of watching a loved one die—too early. We mentally revisit the hospital room when the doctor tactfully reports that our newborn baby has a serious birth defect.

Over time, we wrestle with the question, is God trustworthy? The outward appearance for the situation does not indicate that God intervened in our circumstances. Will we cut and run from our relationship with God, or will we rely on Him and believe His character is still good?

Carol Kent
A New Kind of Normal

Gomer, a Picture of Israel

The LORD said to Hosea, "Go, take to
yourself a wife of harlotry and have
children of harlotry; for the land commits
flagrant harlotry, forsaking the LORD."
So he went and took Gomer the daughter
of Diblaim, and she conceived
and bore him a son.

HOSEA 1:2–3 NASB

Do you have a child who has wandered away from
every good thing you tried to give him? Your
heart has broken as that child perhaps chose a lifestyle
that so contradicted your own. Now imagine God going through this same kind of pain as an entire nation,
one He dearly loved, refused to walk with Him.

Why would God ask the prophet Hosea to enter
into an unwholesome alliance? Because He wanted
Israel to understand what it was like to observe the
one to whom they were betrothed go off and play the
harlot. When Israel entered into the covenant with
God, the people had promised fidelity to Him. But
this beloved nation had "prostituted" themselves in

worship of false gods, forsaking their true God.

The book of Hosea reveals the brokenness of God's own heart as He watched Israel wander away. Now God was forced to take action against the people He loved in order to bring them back to Him.

Carol L. Fitzpatrick
Daily Wisdom for Women

Hope in His Promises

It is better to take refuge in
the LORD than to trust in humans.

PSALM 118:8 NIV

Do it! Choose Jesus Christ! Deny yourself, take up the Cross, and follow Him—for the world must be shown. The world must see, in us, a discernible, visible, startling difference.

Put your trust in Him. Not in people or circumstances or dreams or programs or plans, not in any human notion of what will or won't happen, but in the God of Abraham, Isaac, and Jacob, of Daniel and all the others—the God whose Son went through the darkest valleys so that you and I might be saved. If somebody was willing to give his life for you, would you trust him? Of course you would. Jesus loved you then. He loves you now. He'll be loving you every minute of every hour of every day of the rest of your life, and no matter what happens, nothing can separate you from that love. I know it's true. I have found that sure and steadfast Refuge in my Lord and Savior—the

only real safety—the Everlasting Arms! I've walked
with God a long time. I know He keeps His promises.

Elisabeth Elliot
Secure in the Everlasting Arms

Going through the Fire

So Shadrach, Meshach, and Abednego
stepped out of the fire. Then the
high officers, officials, governors,
and advisers crowded around them and
saw that the fire had not touched them.
Not a hair on their heads was singed,
and their clothing was not scorched.
They didn't even smell of smoke!

DANIEL 3:26–27 NLT

There is a saying when we're going through something really tough—that we're going through the
fire.

It's just a metaphor of course, but it sure describes
the feeling, doesn't it? I know of so many people
lately—dealing with health issues. . .the death of a
loved one. . .job loss. . .marital trouble—so many
people going through the fire.

And it makes me think of those three young
men—Shadrach, Meshach, and Abednego—who went
through real fire.

The thing that has always impressed me about that
story is that they were thrown into the fire bound, but

when they came back out again, only one thing had burned: not their clothes, skin, or hair. No—the only thing that had been burned in the furnace was that which had bound them. They came out *unbound*!

We wonder why the Lord allows us to go through the fire—maybe it's only to destroy that thing that has us bound, too.

Suzie Thomas
Circle of Friends

Soul Food

Jesus answered, "It is written:
'Man shall not live on bread alone,
but on every word that comes
from the mouth of God.' "

MATTHEW 4:4 NIV

At times in my battle with fear and depression I sat down to read the Word of God feeling so depleted, numb, or preoccupied with my mental state that I could hardly even comprehend the words. I not only didn't feel close to God but felt it futile to hope He could ever change me or my life in any lasting way. In spite of that, as I read I was struck by a remarkable lifting of those negative emotions. Afterward I may not have been able to pass a Bible school quiz on the passage, but I felt renewed, strengthened, and hopeful.

When you feel confused, fearful, depressed, or anxious, take the Bible in hand and say, "This book is on my side. My soul is starving, and this is food for my spirit. I want to do the right thing, and reading the Bible is always the right thing to do. Lord, I thank You for Your Word. Reveal Yourself to me as I read it, and let it come alive in my heart and mind. Show me what I need for my life today. Let Your Word penetrate through anything that would block me from receiving it."

Then begin to read until you sense peace coming into your heart.

Stormie Omartian
Finding Peace for Your Heart

Go Forth and Produce

May the favor of the Lord our
God rest on us; establish the
work of our hands for us.

PSALM 90:17 NIV

As sons and daughters of God, we are called to imitate Christ (that is what the word *Christian* means—"Christ-follower") and continue the work of God on earth. We are to finish what He started, which is to be fruitful and productive in whatever field we find ourselves in.

As you strive to complete the work placed in your hands, you should find delight and fulfillment in it. If you are an administrator, you should be thriving on the details of your work, flourishing as you supervise others with grace and authority. If you are an artist, your creativity—the things God has placed within you to express—should surprise you!

No matter what your profession, it should reveal your strengths to you—as well as your weaknesses, the areas that could use improvement and refining. All of this is how we bless others and glorify God as we grow into a greater reflection of His creative power. Understanding that we are literally the extension of God's arms to the world is huge. Our inherent talents or gifts actually make up the expression of His care for those on earth.

Michelle McKinney Hammond
How to Make Life Work

Hope in His Name

"I am the Alpha and the Omega,"
says the Lord God, "who is, and who
was, and who is to come, the Almighty."

REVELATION 1:8 NIV

In the Gospel of John Christ adopts this name of "I am" as His own. These simple words, I am, express eternity and unchangeableness of existence, which is the very first element necessary in a God who is to be depended upon. No dependence could be placed by any one of us upon a changeable God. He must be the same yesterday, today, and forever, if we are to have any peace or comfort.

But is this all His name implies, simply "I am"? I am what? we ask. What does this "I am" include? It includes everything the human heart longs for and needs. This unfinished name of God seems to me like a blank check signed by a rich friend given to us to be filled in with whatever sum we may desire. The whole Bible tells us what it means. Every attribute of God, every revelation of His character, every proof of His undying love, every declaration of His watchful care, every assertion of His purposes of tender mercy, every manifestation of His loving kindness—all are the filling out of this unfinished "I am." God tells us through all the pages of His Book what He is. "I am," He says, "I am all that my people need"; "I am their strength"; "I am their wisdom"; "I am their righteousness"; "I am their peace"; "I am their salvation"; "I am their life"; "I am their all in all!"

This apparently unfinished name, therefore, is the most comforting name the heart of man could devise, because it allows us to add to it, without any limitation, whatever we feel the need of, and even "exceeding abundantly" beyond all that we can ask or think.

Hannah Whitall Smith
The God of All Comfort

Futile Faith?

> "My righteous ones will live by faith.
> But I will take no pleasure in
> anyone who turns away."

HEBREWS 10:38 NLT

We clean the windows and wash the car, and a day later it rains. We sweep the kitchen floor, and hours later the crunch of cookie crumbs resounds under our feet. Some tasks seem so futile.

So it is with our spiritual life. We pray unceasingly and no answers seem to come, or we work tirelessly and problems entrench us. In frustration we wonder, *Why did this happen? What purpose is there to all of this?* It all seems so pointless.

To the skeptic, logic must pervade every situation. If not, there is no basis for belief. But to the person of faith, logic gives way to faith—especially during the most tumultuous, nonsensical times.

So even when our prayers remain unanswered, we continue to pray. Even when God is silent, we continue to believe. And though we grope for answers, we continue to trust.

When our chaotic lives turn upside down and we labor to find rhyme and reason, God asks us to hold fast to our faith. For no labor of love is pointless; no prayer is futile.

Tina Krause
Whispers of Wisdom for Busy Women

He Is All We Need

Whom have I in heaven but
you? And earth has nothing
I desire besides you.

PSALM 73:25 NIV

Growing is not always easy, but it is the only way to blossom.

I find many people today who are looking for things that offer a certain measure of self-esteem and self-confidence in a variety of places—a job, spouse, higher education, etc. And while these things are good, they only offer limited satisfaction. Others seek self-esteem or fulfillment in the wrong places. They look for love, but they look for it in an affair. They seek security but seek it in a mate, job, or stock portfolio. They long for a sense of peace and serenity but seek it in a bottle of alcohol or pills. They desire self-esteem, so they acquire possessions and status symbols. One of the greatest examples Mother has been to me is of a woman who has not looked to anything or anyone to be to her what only Jesus Christ can be.

You see, all we need and desire, He is. At some point in each of our lives, God will bring us to a place where He will prove this to us.

Gigi Graham Tchividjian
A Quiet Knowing

God Loves You—Flaws and All

So let's come near God with
pure hearts and a confidence
that comes from having faith.

HEBREWS 10:22 CEV

If you listen closely, you can hear them. Women around the globe, groaning and moaning in dressing rooms. Are they in pain? Are they ill? No, it's just bathing suit season, and they're trying to find the one perfect suit that doesn't make them look fat. It's a quest every woman embarks on, and it's one of the most daunting tasks she will ever face.

Seriously, is there anything more humbling than standing in front of a dressing room mirror, under those unforgiving fluorescent lights, trying on bathing suit after bathing suit? While you might be able to hide a few dimples underneath blue jeans or a nice black dress, you're not hiding anything in a bathing suit.

That's pretty much how it is with God. You might be able to fake grin your way through church. But when you enter the throne room, it's like wearing your bathing suit before God. You can't hide any imperfections from Him.

Here's the great thing about God. He gave us Jesus to take care of our sin, because God knew we'd be flawed. We can't earn our way into God's favor. All we have to do is ask Jesus to be the Lord of our lives, and we're "in." Then, whenever we enter the throne room, God sees us through "the Jesus filter," and all He sees is perfection. Now if we could just figure out some kind of perfection filter for bathing suit season, life would be super.

Michelle Medlock Adams

Secrets of Beauty

The Power of Prayer

I will give you thanks, for you answered
me; you have become my salvation.

PSALM 118:21 NIV

I heard about a terrible criminal who had just been
condemned to death for some horrible crimes. Everything would lead one to believe that he would die
without repenting. I wanted at all cost to prevent him
from going to hell. In order to do that I used every
imaginable means: Sensing that in myself I could do
nothing, I offered to God all the infinite merits of Our
Lord and the treasures of the Holy Church. Finally
I begged [my aunt] to have a Mass said for my intentions. Deep in my heart I felt certainty that my desires
would be granted, but in order to give myself courage
to continue to pray for sinners, I told God that I was
quite sure that He would forgive the poor miserable
criminal, and that I would believe this even if he did
not confess and showed no sign of repentance, so
much did I have confidence in Jesus' infinite mercy,
but I asked Him only for "a sign" of repentance simply
for my consolation. . . .

My prayer was granted to the letter! I put my hand on the newspaper *La Croix*. I opened it hurriedly, and what did I see? . . . Oh! My tears betrayed my emotion, and I was obliged to go hide. . . . The criminal had not confessed; he had climbed up onto the scaffold and was getting ready to put his head into the ominous opening in the guillotine, when suddenly, gripped with a sudden inspiration, he turned back, grabbed a crucifix that the priest was holding up to him, and kissed its sacred wounds three times! Then his soul went to receive the merciful judgment of the One who declares that in heaven there will be more joy for a single sinner who repents than for ninety-nine righteous persons who have no need for repentance! (Luke 15:7).

Saint Therese of Lisieux
The Story of a Soul

The Power of Unity

Now the multitude of those who believed
were of one heart and one soul. . .
And with great power the apostles gave
witness to the resurrection of the Lord
Jesus. And great grace was upon them all.

ACTS 4:32–33 NKJV

The ultimate power of prayer is found in a church where people of one mind unite.

The need to come together is an integral part of our makeup. In Genesis we read, "The LORD God said, It is not good that the man should be alone" (2:18 KJV). We were *created* to come together before God. When Jesus taught us how to pray, He didn't begin with "*My* Father which art in heaven" but "*Our* Father which art in heaven."

The evidence of the power of gathering and praying in one accord is staggering! And it's not only the power felt amid Christ's presence, but the joy of a holy fellowship!

The church is where the Word of God is taught, spiritual direction gleaned, and encouragement given. The body of Christ is a living body that serves a living

God. And it is a place of power only when we are united, seeking and moving together in His will.

The church is the place where we are all reminded of the power of unity under God. It is where our focus is to be solely on the heavens above, a place where we gather with one common purpose—to love God and each other. In such a spiritual haven, fellow believers are pulled away from earthly concerns and look to Christ seated in the heavenlies with God. There is no greater joy!

Donna K. Maltese
Power Prayers to Start Your Day

Depend on Him

"Ask and it will be given to you;
seek and you will find; knock and
the door will be opened to you."

MATTHEW 7:7 NIV

O My children, what do you need today? Is it comfort; is it courage; is it healing; is it guidance? Lo, I say unto thee, that whatever it is that ye need, if ye will look to Me, I will supply.

I will be to thee what the sun is to the flower; what the water of the ocean is to the fish; and what the sky is to the birds. For I will be the giver to thee of life and light and strength. I will surround thee and preserve thee, so that in Me ye may live, move, and have your being, existing in Me when apart from Me ye would die. Yea, I will be to thee as the wide open skies, in that I will liberate thy spirit in such fashion that ye shall not be earthbound.

Ye shall live in a realm where the things of earth shall not be able to impede and obstruct and limit thy movement; but ye shall be freed in Me to a place where thy spirit may soar as the eagle, and ye may make your nest in a place of safety and solitude, unmolested and undefiled by the sordidness of the world.

Thou shalt have companionship; but it shall be the companionship of those like-minded with thee, yea, of those who like thyself have been done with the beggarly elements, and whose sense of value has been readjusted so that they deem the unseen as of greater value than the seen, and the spiritual riches more precious than the wealth of the world.

Be done with petty things. Be done with small dreams. Give Me all that you have and are; and I will share with you abundantly all that I have and all that I am.

Frances J. Roberts
Come Away My Beloved

Holding On

We should remove from our lives
anything that would get in the way and
the sin that so easily holds us back.

HEBREWS 12:1 NCV

I saw a television show that both fascinated and
repelled me. It was about hoarders; that is, people
who are unable to throw anything away. I found out
that it's not that they *want* to live this way—they are
unable to force themselves to make decisions and
things just pile up on them, literally.

One dear man could not get the door to his one-
room efficiency apartment shut. In another lady's
house her "stuff" had piled up to shoulder height *in
every room*! Eventually she was simply overwhelmed by
the enormous task of deciding what to keep and what
to throw away.

It made me pause to wonder if I'm not more like
these precious people than I would like to admit. Am
I hoarding things in my spiritual life—holding on to
shattered dreams and unfulfilled plans, unable to let
go of old hurts and wounds, salvaging every scrap of

disappointment or heartache, or piling up justifications for my attitude and responses to other people? Have I let the mess of my sins drop on the floor of my life, afraid to let go or allow God to have full rein and clean me up?

As with the people who sought out help to clean up their homes, it is a process that takes the support of someone with the ability to help untangle the mess. Spiritually speaking, that's our Helper, the Holy Spirit.

Missy Horsfall
Circle of Friends

Jehovah-Tsidkenu

"For the time is coming," says the LORD, "when I will raise up a righteous descendant from King David's line. He will be a King who rules with wisdom. He will do what is just and right throughout the land. And this will be his name: 'The LORD Is Our Righteousness.' In that day Judah will be saved, and Israel will live in safety."

JEREMIAH 23:5–6 NLT

Many of us look back to the good old days. But Israel was told by Jeremiah to look forward to the good new days that lay ahead. Jehovah Himself would provide not only a lamb for an atoning sacrifice, but a hope for the future. Psychologists tell us people cannot function without hope. Yet many people today feel a hopelessness that never seems to go away.

Without Christ there is no hope for the future because He is the future. God holds the future as surely as He holds the past and the present. He is working His purposes out. He knows the plans that He has for us: plans of good and not of disaster. Without God, without Christ, without hope, we are lost people groping in the dark for some meaning to life.

"The time is coming," says the Lord, when He will provide one who will put all things in their proper place. Rights will be respected and wrongs redressed. There will be salvation and security for God's people. This is our hope. There's a new day coming for the believer.

Jehovah-Tsidkenu gives us that new day, that hope, that future. Do you feel hopeless? "Hope in God" (Psalm 42:5 NLT).

Jill Briscoe
The One Year Book of Devotions for Women

The Will to Fulfill

And there we saw the giants, the sons of
Anak, which come of the giants: and we
were in our own sight as grasshoppers,
and so we were in their sight.

NUMBERS 13:33 KJV

The ten fearful spies who joined Caleb on the trip into Canaan may have had what we'd call a poor self-image. Compared to the Canaanites, they seemed to be small potatoes—grasshoppers even! And they imagined that their enemies would see them as these irritating insects. When the Israelite spies described themselves that way, they were relying on their own power. And looking at it from that perspective, they were probably right. They didn't have the ability to overthrow people who had cities and villages in Canaan. The Canaanites were entrenched in the land, and moving them out was a big project.

Unlike Caleb and Joshua, these men didn't consider doing the job under God's power. They forgot who had led them there and what He'd promised them.

When you feel like a grasshopper compared to

coworkers, huge projects, or anything else, are you looking at yourself through the right lens? Are you seeing your working life through God's eyes or your own?

Lord, lead me in my working life. I know You've brought me here for a reason, and I want to fulfill Your will.

Pamela L. McQuade
Daily Wisdom for the Workplace

His Good Work in You

And I am certain that God, who began
the good work within you, will continue
his work until it is finally finished on the
day when Christ Jesus returns.

PHILIPPIANS 1:6 NLT

Do you have an impossible job to do? Has the
Lord told you to do it? Go ahead! When we
pray, we enter God's domain from the domain of our
inability. He is conqueror and makes us more than
conquerors. It is not bad if we feel weak, if our inability is a reality to us. That's exactly when the Lord
does miracles. Paul said, "When I am weak, then I am
strong." Do you know why I thought it so important
that these people in that country learned to forgive?
Jesus said that if we do not forgive, we will not be
forgiven, and we break down the bridge that we need
for ourselves. Jesus is coming again very soon, and
we must be prepared—by being in good relationship
with God and with others. We can't get it together
ourselves, however hard we try. But if we place our
weak hand in the strong hand of Jesus, then He does

it. Jesus is looking forward to His return to earth and it is He who is preparing us for His return. Surrender to Him completely. He who began a good work in you will bring it to completion on that day—the day of His Second Coming.

Corrie ten Boom
Reflections of God's Glory

Persistence

"For the past twenty-three years. . .the
LORD has been giving me his messages.
I have faithfully passed them on to you."

JEREMIAH 25:3 NLT

The Bible is full of persistent people, people who persevered despite problems and difficulties, long after the time most people would consider such persistence wise. Noah spent one hundred years building the ark. Abraham waited twenty-five years for Isaac, the son of promise. And by the end of his life, Jeremiah had preached God's message to an unbelieving audience for forty years. Israelites called him a traitor, threw him in prison, and left him to die, but he continued preaching God's message. Nothing slowed him down.

Jeremiah's faith enabled him to persevere. The writer of Hebrews could have had Jeremiah in mind when he wrote, "Some faced. . .chains and imprisonment. . . . They went about. . .destitute, persecuted and mistreated—the world was not worthy of them" (Hebrews 11:36–38 NIV).

God expects the same persistence of us. He calls for persistence, also known as perseverance, over a dozen times in the New Testament. He means for the trials that come our way to increase our perseverance. When we successfully pass small hurdles, He may put bigger ones in our way. Why? Because He doesn't love us? No—because He does.

Persistence results in faith that is pure, molten gold.

Darlene Franklin
Whispers of Wisdom for Busy Women

Contributors

MICHELLE MEDLOCK ADAMS has a diverse résumé featuring inspirational books, children's picture books, and greeting cards. Her insights have appeared in periodicals across America, including *Today's Christian Woman* and *Guideposts for Kids*. She lives in Fort Worth, Texas with her husband, two daughters, and a "mini petting zoo."

EMILY BIGGERS is a gifted education specialist in a north Texas public school district. She enjoys travel, freelance writing, and serving in a local apartment ministry through her church.

JOANNA BLOSS is a personal trainer, writer, and student living in the Midwest. She is a coauthor of *Grit for the Oyster: 250 Pearls of Wisdom for Aspiring Authors*.

CORRIE TEN BOOM was simply an ordinary, middle-aged Dutch spinster when the Second World War began. By the time the conflict ended, she was literally transformed by the faith she had merely accepted, and on a mission from God. By God's grace, Corrie survived the concentration camp and became a "tramp for the Lord," sharing in more than sixty nations the thrilling message that nothing, not even death, can separate us from God's love.

JILL BRISCOE is the author of more than forty books—including devotionals, study guides, poetry, and children's books. She serves as executive editor of *Just Between Us* magazine and served on the board of World Relief and *Christianity Today* for more than twenty years. Jill and her husband make their home in Milwaukee, Wisconsin.

AMY CARMICHAEL (1867–1951) was a Protestant Christian missionary in India who opened an orphanage and founded a mission in Dohnavur. She served in India for fifty-six years without furlough and authored many books about her missionary work.

FANNY CROSBY (1820–1915), blinded in infancy, became one of the most popular and prolific of all hymn writers. She wrote more than eight thousand hymns in her lifetime, including the best-known "Blessed Assurance," "Jesus Is Tenderly Calling You Home," "Praise Him, Praise Him," and "To God Be the Glory."

NANCY LEIGH DEMOSS grew up in a family deeply committed to Christ and to the mission of world evangelization. Today, Nancy mentors millions of women through Revive Our Hearts and the True Woman Movement, calling them to heart revival and biblical womanhood. Her books have sold more than two million copies and include *Lies Women Believe* and *A Thirty-Day Walk with God in the Psalms*. She also coauthored *Seeking Him* and *Lies Young Women Believe* and is the general editor of *Becoming God's True Woman*.

DENA DYER is a writer who resides in the Texas Hill Country. She has contributed to more than a dozen anthologies and has authored or coauthored three humor books. Find out more about Dena at www.denadyer.com.

TINA C. ELACQUA teaches, writes, and publishes journal articles, books, conference papers and presentations, and technical reports/presentations. She has held roles of research scientist, professor, and consultant in industrial/organizational psychology.

ELISABETH ELLIOT is a best-selling author of more than twenty books including *Passion and Purity, Be Still My Soul, The Path of Loneliness,* and *Keep a Quiet Heart*. She and her husband, Lars Gren, make their home in Magnolia, Massachusetts.

SUZANNE WOODS FISHER's historical novels, *Copper Star* and its sequel, *Copper Fire,* are inspired by true events. Fisher writes for many magazines, is a wife and mother, and is a puppy raiser for Guide Dogs for the Blind.

CAROL L. FITZPATRICK is a bestselling author of nine books that have totaled nearly three quarters of a million books sold. She is a frequent conference speaker for writing groups and church groups. Carol and her husband have three grown children and three grandchildren. Although she credits her Midwest upbringing for instilling her core values, she has lived in California for nearly four decades.

DARLENE FRANKLIN lives in Englewood, Colorado. She is the author of several romance novels for Barbour's Heartsong Presents! series, as well as the *Dressed for Death* mystery series and numerous articles. You may visit her website at www.darlenefranklin.com.

MICHELLE MCKINNEY HAMMOND is a bestselling author, speaker, singer, and television cohost. She has authored more than thirty books including bestselling titles *The Diva Principle; Sassy, Single, and Satisfied; 101 Ways to Get and Keep His Attention;* and *Secrets of an Irresistible Woman*. She makes her home in Chicago.

JOCELYN HAMSHER is a gifted Bible study teacher, writer, board member, and speaker for Circle of Friends Ministries. She lives in Sugarcreek, Ohio, with her husband, Bruce, and their three sons. She enjoys spending time with family, studying the Word of God, drinking coffee, and laughing with her husband.

JANICE HANNA, who lives in the Houston area, writes novels, nonfiction, magazine articles, and musical comedies for the stage. The mother of four married daughters, she is quickly adding grandchildren to the family mix.

LISA HARPER is an excellent communicator, author, speaker, and Bible teacher. She has spoken at Women of Faith, Moody Bible, Winsome Women, and Focus on the Family conferences and has written a number of books including *A Perfect Mess: How God Adores and Transforms Imperfect People Like Us*.

FRANCES RIDLEY HAVERGAL (1836–1879) was an English poet and hymn writer. "Take My Life and Let It Be" is one of her best-known hymns. She also wrote hymn melodies, religious tracts, and works for children.

KIM HILL is a Grammy-nominated, multi-Dove-award-winning singer and songwriter. Worship leader, speaker, and author of the devotional book *Hope No Matter What* and companion CD, Kim's other releases include *Surrender, Real Christmas, Surrounded By Mercy, and Broken Things*.

MISSY HORSFALL is a published magazine and greeting card writer and coauthor of the novel *Double Honor*. A pastor's wife, she is a speaker and Bible study teacher for Circle of Friends and serves on the board overseeing writing ministries. Missy also produces and cohosts the COF radio program.

JULIE HUFSTETLER is a singer, songwriter, and worship leader who encourages and connects with listeners, whether she's singing alongside recording artist Mark Schultz or with noted speakers like Sheila Walsh, Dee Brestin, and Nancy Leigh DeMoss. She and her husband, Guy, live in northeast Ohio with their three sons.

SHARON JAYNES is the author of thirteen books with Harvest House Publishers, Focus on the Family, and Moody Publishers and a frequent guest on national radio and television. She has also written numerous magazine articles and devotions for publications such as *Focus on the Family, Decision, In Touch*, and Crosswalk.com.

BARBARA JOHNSON, (1927–2007), was an award-winning author and Women of Faith Speaker Emeritus with more than four million books in print and translated into ten foreign languages. She faced her long battle with cancer with the same humor and wisdom she met the many adversities of her life.

AUSTINE KELLER resides in Tampa, Florida, writing and publishing as a ministry to others as well as for her own enjoyment. She also enjoys a newly emptied nest and fishing with her husband.

CAROL KENT is an internationally known speaker and author. Her books include *When I Lay My Isaac Down, Becoming a Woman of Influence,* and *Mothers Have Angel Wings.* She is president of Speak Up Speaker Services and the founder and director of Speak Up With Confidence seminars.

VIRELLE KIDDER is a full-time writer and conference speaker and author of six books including *Meet Me at the Well* and *The Best Life Ain't Easy.* She is published in national magazines such as *Moody Magazine, Focus on the Family's Pastor's Family, Decision, Pray!, Journey, HomeLife,* and *Tapestry.*

TINA KRAUSE is an award-winning newspaper columnist and author of the book *Laughter Therapy.* She is a wife, mom, and grandmother of five. Tina and her husband, Jim, live in Valparaiso, Indiana.

DONNA K. MALTESE is a freelance writer, editor, and proofreader; publicist for a local Mennonite project; and the assistant director of RevWriter Writers Conferences. Donna resides in Bucks County, Pennsylvania, with her husband and two children. She is a pastor's prayer partner and is active in her local church.

PAMELA L. MCQUADE is a freelance writer and editor in Nutley, New Jersey, who has worked with numerous publishers. Her Barbour credits include *The Word on Life, Daily Wisdom for Couples,* and *Prayers and Promises,* all coauthored with Toni Sortor. Pam and her husband share their home with basset hounds and are involved in basset hound rescue.

HELEN WIDGER MIDDLEBROOKE is a homemaker, home educator, and mother of nine. She is a freelance columnist and the author of *Lessons for a Supermom* (Barbour Publishing, 2002).

JANINE MILLER grew up in Holmes County, Ohio. She currently homeschools her children, ages five to fifteen, and works part-time from her home as a church secretary. Janine and her husband of twenty-three years live in southern Ohio with their four children.

MANDY NYDEGGER lives with her husband, David, in Waco, Texas. She loves Christmas, snow, and the Indianapolis Colts.

NICOLE O'DELL, wife and mother of three, is an accomplished writer of books, devotions, and Bible studies. She has been a Bible study leader and teacher for over fifteen years.

STORMIE OMARTIAN is a popular writer, speaker, and author. She is author of the bestselling *The Power of Praying*® books as well as many other titles. She and her husband have been married thirty years and have three grown children.

DONNA PARTOW is an author and motivational speaker. Her books, including *This Isn't The Life I Signed Up For...but I'm Finding Hope and Healing* and *Becoming A Vessel God Can Use*, have sold almost a million copies, and her ministry Pieces4Peace reaches into the largest Muslim city in the world.

ELIZABETH PRENTISS (1818–1878) was the daughter of an early nineteenth-century revival preacher and began writing as a teenager. Born in 1818 in Portland, Maine, Prentiss was also the writer of the hymn "More Love to Thee, O Christ." Prentiss died in Vermont in 1878.

SARAH MAE RATLIFF enjoys worshipping God, writing, working with children, and spending time with her family. Sarah and her husband, Ryan, are high school sweethearts who welcomed their first son into the world in April of 2013.

JULIE RAYBURN is a public speaker and an area director for Community Bible Study. She lives in Atlanta with her husband, Scott. They have two grown children and one granddaughter.

BECKI REISER is wife to Jeff and mother to three grown boys and one daughter. After the murder of their seventeen-year-old daughter, Jeff and Becki began a ministry of sharing their testimony of forgiveness. Becki is a contributing author in Standard Publishing's Devotions magazine and Circle of Friends website, www.ourcircleoffriends.org.

RAMONA RICHARDS is a freelance writer and editor living in Tennessee. Formerly the editor of Ideals magazine, Ramona has also edited children's books, fiction, nonfiction, study Bibles, and reference books for major Christian publishers. She is the author of A Moment with God for Single Parents.

BOBBIE RILL is a motivational speaker and life coach. As a licensed professional counselor, she served as executive director over a multistate network of Christian counseling and educational centers. She also directed Women of Virtue, a national conference and radio ministry. She and her husband, Bob, reside in Tucson, Arizona.

FRANCES J. ROBERTS (1918–2009) is best known for her classic devotional *Come Away My Beloved*. She founded The King's Press in 1964, where she authored and published *Come Away* and eight other books, selling over 1.5 million copies in the last thirty years.

LEAH SLAWSON has been married to her husband, Guice, for more than twenty years and they have two teenagers, a son and daughter. She lives in Montgomery, Alabama.

EMILY SMITH lives in Greenfield, Indiana, with her wonderful husband, Eric. Married for two years, the only children they currently have are four-legged. Emily works for a home health agency and is a weekly blogger for the Circle of Friends website. She loves reading, cooking, and spending time with family.

HANNAH WHITALL SMITH (1832–1911) was born into a strict Quaker home in Philadelphia and became a major influence in the Holiness movement of the late nineteenth century. Besides *The Christian's Secret of a Happy Life*, Smith also wrote *The God of All Comfort* and an autobiography, *The Unselfishness of God and How I Discovered It*.

JOYCE STRONG is an author and international conference speaker whose books include *Journey to Joy; Leading With Passion* and *Grace; Instruments for His Glory; Lambs on the Ledge; Caught in the Crossfire; Of Dreams and Kings and Mystical Things; A Dragon, A Dreamer, and The Promise Giver*.

GIGI GRAHAM TCHIVIDJIAN, daughter of Billy and Ruth Graham, is a busy wife, mother, grandmother, author, and speaker. She currently writes a regular column for *Christian Parenting* magazine and has written four books, including *Weather of the Heart* and *A Search for Serenity*.

LYSA TERKEURST is a nationally known speaker and president of Proverbs 31 Ministry. An award-winning author of twelve books, including *Becoming More Than a Good Bible Study Girl,* she has been featured on Focus on the Family, Family Life Today, *Good Morning America*, and in *Woman's Day* magazine.

SAINT THERESE OF LISIEUX (1873–1897) became a French Carmelite nun at the age of fifteen. Her memoir, *Story of a Soul,* inspired thousands to recognize God's unique call on their lives. She was canonized by Pope Pius XI in 1925.

SUZIE THOMAS serves Malone University as director of university relations and editor of *The Malone Magazine.* Author of *Read It Again Bible Stories: The Miracles of Jesus,* Suzie has a bachelor's degree in education and a master's in communication. She also has experience as a producer and radio host.

SHEILA WALSH is a unique combination of international author, speaker, worship leader, television talk show host, and Bible teacher. She is a speaker with Women of Faith and bestselling author of her memoir *Honestly* and the Gold Medallion Award nominee for *The Heartache No One Sees*.

Permissions